# AIR RIFLE HUNTING THROUGH THE SEASONS

## A Guide to Fieldcraft

# Mathew Manning

McNIDDER | &
GRACE

Published by McNidder & Grace
4 Chapel Lane, Alnwick, NE66 1XT

A catalogue record for this book is available from the British Library

ISBN: 978-0-85716-033-1

Photographs by Mathew Manning and Kevin Hawker

Illustrations by Matt Donovan

Designed by Obsidian Design

Printed in Malta on behalf of Latitude Press Limited

For Grandad Hawker

# THANKS

Sally, George and Violet.

Kev Hawker, Nigel Allen, Jeffrey Olstead, Mike Montgomery, Joe Dimbleby, Tim Dunning, Mike Appleby, Ian Barnett, Fanny Charles and the Blackmore Vale Media editorial team, Andy Peden Smith, Matt Donovan, Andrew Hall, Malc Barnard, Barry Hutchins, Gareth Ham, Tony Belas, Roe Norman, Edward Thring, The House family at Yarlington, Bob Down, Jamie Ransome, Tony Gibson, Wes Stanton, Peter Carr, Terry Doe, Matt Clark, Jed Woodhouse, Blaze Publishing, Airgun Shooter magazine, Shooting Times magazine, Sporting Rifle magazine, Shooting and Conservation magazine, Air Gunner magazine, the British Association for Shooting and Conservation (BASC), Daystate, Deben, BSA Guns, Hawke Optics, Weihrauch, Hull Cartridge, the Honeycombe Shoot, Kingweston Estate, Tower Guns and Mendip Shooting Ground.

# CONTENTS

# FOREWORD

Some people buy an air rifle especially to control pests, others, having honed their skills on paper targets, look for something more challenging. However you approach live quarry shooting, it certainly is challenging and adds a huge new dimension to your sport. We can't all afford to stalk a Highland stag but you'd be surprised at the skill it takes to stalk a hedgerow rabbit – and how satisfying a successful stalk can be.

Quite apart from the extra shooting skills that need to be learned there is the supreme challenge of fieldcraft. Getting to know your quarry, think like it and above all respect it.

It will take a lifetime to acquire those skills but with this book you are off to a flying start.

Years of experience are distilled into simple advice that will save you many hours of frustration and help you to get the fullest enjoyment from a truly challenging and engrossing sport. Air gunning is not only the most accessible form of shooting but it is arguably the most beneficial – everything you legally shoot is a pest. So read this book, learn the lessons and enjoy some great sport.

**Jeffrey Olstead**
*Head of Publications*
*British Association for Shooting and Conservation*

# INTRODUCTION

Hunting with air rifles is one of the most effective, rewarding and accessible methods of shooting, whether for pest control or the pot. The modern air rifle is quiet and accurate, and suffers less of the restrictions that hamper the ownership and use of more powerful weapons. What's more, the air rifle hunter's quarry species – from rabbits and grey squirrels to pigeons and magpies – are regarded as pests. Rather than paying through the nose for the chance to shoot reared game on some grand estate, the airgun shooter is often called upon to control pests that are causing problems for farmers, gamekeepers and foresters, so shooting usually comes for free.

By and large, air rifle hunting is widely available and easily accessible. And, if you're setting your sights on rabbits or pigeons, there's the added bonus of a free meal made with some of the tastiest and healthiest free-range meat you could wish for.

Accessible as it may be, the right to shoot should always be regarded as a privilege that is paid for by showing respect for your quarry. The air rifle hunter out controlling rats and feral pigeons on the farm shares the same obligation to ensure a swift, humane death for his quarry as the stalker pursuing deer on the hill. Compared with the stalker, the airgun shooter is feebly armed but the tool of his trade is deadly accurate. Modern air rifles are capable of grouping shots inside a circle the size of your thumbnail at ranges of up to 50 metres, and beyond; it is the shooter who provides the weakest link in the chain. Discipline and self-control are vital attributes, for the air rifle hunter must hone his skills on the target range and then, depending on his ability and conditions on the day, decide when to take or leave a shot at live quarry.

But long-range marksmanship is not the be-all and end-all of hunting with air rifles – far from it. The greatest skill, and greatest thrill, of this engaging sport is getting close to your quarry. By mastering the art of fieldcraft and understanding the habits and foibles of the wild creatures he wishes to target, the air rifle hunter will undoubtedly enjoy greater success in the field. Mastering the 50-metre shot is beyond the abilities of many, but getting to within 25 metres of your quarry is achievable by more or less anyone who's prepared to learn.

My first book, *Hunting with Air Rifles – The Complete Guide*, provides an overview of all aspects of the sport: from choosing your gun, clothing and ammunition, becoming a proficient shot and understanding the law of airgun ownership, to hunting techniques, game preparation and cooking recipes. Some of the passages on airgun law and ethical hunting are echoed in the following pages, and for that I make no apology. Although they may not be the most exciting chapters, they contain vital information to keep you on the right side of the law. The main intention of this book, however, is to delve deeper into the lore of fieldcraft – the deadliest weapon in any hunter's arsenal.

Unlocking the secrets of the relationship between wildlife, the countryside and the ever-changing seasons is what separates a good hunter from a great hunter. Unlike the pheasant shooter, the air rifle hunter has to pit his wits against the finely-tuned senses of wild creatures that run the gauntlet of survival every day. These animals don't have the luxury of a protective gamekeeper to provide their meals and eradicate the species that prey on them. The wild animals the airgun shooter targets live on their wits to avoid the perils of predation and starvation on a daily basis. That is why they are so wary and cunning.

The habits of wild creatures – quarry species included – tend to be dictated by the urge to feed, breed and survive, and the way they achieve this is greatly influenced by seasonal changes, which include the weather and the availability of food. These patterns change with the seasons – and often far more frequently. The annual cycle includes the hot, dry days of summer, the abundance of the autumn harvest, the harsh days of winter and the return of life to the countryside in the spring. Knowing how to predict animals' reactions to these changes enables the hunter to ensure that he's in the right place at the right time.

Why are fields that were grey with woodpigeons yesterday deserted today? Why do I never see rabbits in the fields where I shoot despite the obvious signs of their presence? The answers to such questions are obvious when you understand the changing patterns of the countryside and the creatures that live in it. Nature provides all the necessary clues – it's just a case of knowing where to find them and how to read them.

Through this book, I hope to provide a seasonal guide that will help you not only to pre-empt what your quarry is doing and where it's doing it, but also to ensure that you have a deeper understanding of fieldcraft. This refers collectively to the skills – from stalking and ambushing to hide building and decoying – that enable a hunter to fully exploit opportunities when they arise. To me, fieldcraft also refers to a state of mind or, more specifically, trying to think like your quarry would. Through observation and experience, you should be able to adopt the mindset of the wild creatures that you pursue, and therefore give yourself a better chance of pre-empting their whereabouts, their strengths and, most importantly, any weaknesses that you might be able to exploit.

Of course, like so many things in life, hunting trips don't always go exactly to plan. Sometimes nothing seems to work and sometimes you get lucky, but I like to think the harder you try, the luckier you get.

# SPRING

*It's always a pleasure to spend time in the countryside during the spring months.*
*The days are getting longer and warmer, and the extra sunlight teases out*
*the first early blooms from bulbs and blossom and then a lush new covering of fresh green*
*foliage in the woods and hedgerows.*

*As idyllic as English springtime can be, the villains of the countryside will be*
*up to their mischief: magpies and crows will be hunting out easy pickings from the nests of*
*songbirds, and grey squirrels will be doing the same – plus stripping bark from trees*
*to further supplement their diet with sweet, syrupy sap. The hunter's springtime priorities*
*are more likely to lean towards pest control than filling the pot.*

# Outwitting corvids with an owl decoy

Springtime always brings a frenzy of activity to the countryside. The gradually warming rays of sunshine have at last broken the grip of winter, bringing a flush of new growth and a flurry of nesting activity. It's not all sweetness and light, though; survival of the strongest is the natural world's mantra throughout the year and scavengers (corvids in particular) will be raiding the new nests in search of a free meal.

The corvid family is a cunning and villainous clan, and the eggs and young of songbirds form a large part of their diet. Crows and magpies are the worst offenders and, being such intelligent birds, they quickly learn to exploit this protein-rich food source as the nesting season gets underway in spring.

Look along prominent trees in the hedgerow or on the woodland edge, and you'll see corvids sat like silent sentries. As well as looking out for danger, these birds are also studying the routines of their neighbours. They'll have noticed the hen blackbird flitting back and forth to dense shrubs with nesting material in her beak. When the strands of grass are replaced by worms and grubs, the corvids will drop in for a closer investigation in the hope of finding that precious clutch of turquoise eggs. Sometimes crows and magpies are more patient and wait until they can hear the calls of hungry chicks – they know that fledglings make for an even more nourishing meal than eggs.

Anyone who harbours any doubt about the threat that crows and magpies pose to other birds should study their beak and talons. The beak of these corvids is broad and powerful; perfectly adapted for smashing eggshells to expose their contents, for disembowelling even fairly large fledglings, and for tearing through the flesh of weak young lambs. Their claws are long, curved and sharp; evolved as much for tackling prey as for clinging to branches or scratching around for worms and beetles. Crows and magpies will often use their strong claws to secure their prey while that powerful, stabbing beak gets to work. Sheep farmers will vouch for the fact that these tools make short work of the tender flesh of newborn lambs.

Intensive farming and the continual loss of wildlife habitat to housing and industrial development means that wild songbirds in particular need all the help they can get these days. Ironically, scavenging birds such as crows and magpies tend to do better close to man than many other bird species – you've probably seen them grabbing the biggest chunks of bread from your bird table before the smaller birds get a look-in. In fact, corvids positively thrive in urban fringe areas where they get fat on man's waste – scavenging from refuse sacks and any other free meals they happen across. In this environment, they cause even more devastation to struggling songbird colonies, which already have to contend with domestic cats and a perilous lack of habitat. Add to this the costly damage caused to commercial shoots when the vulnerable eggs and chicks of ground-nesting pheasants and partridges succumb to greedy corvids, and there's a clear case for controlling numbers of these devious pests.

The one thing that strikes me when I talk to other shooters is the fact that many of them have such a high regard for the intelligence of crows and magpies that they tend to feel beaten before they even start. While I certainly agree that corvids are incredibly clever birds and are about the most cunning air rifle quarry you could expect to encounter, there are plenty of ways for the thinking shooter to outwit them.

Most importantly, and in spite of all the folklore that surrounds them, we must remember that corvids are *only* birds – albeit very artful birds. Some shooters I have met talk as if crows and magpies do nothing except read shooting books and magazines. These people appear to be under the illusion that corvids know every trick the shooter has up his sleeve and that they spend every waking minute worrying about being shot – they don't.

Relative to most birds, corvids do tend to work things out pretty quickly. They *do* have a strong survival instinct and, from my experiences, they certainly seem to be able to recognise a danger if they've managed to escape it in the past. We hunters need to keep sight of the fact that corvids' strong instincts can also be their downfall, and that we, or most of us, are capable of being far more artful and cunning than any bird.

But corvids don't just face danger in the shape of humans; they run the gauntlet against natural predators. And, because they are habitual nest-robbers, corvids are well aware of the threat that predatory birds pose to their own broods. Consequently, they become incredibly territorial at this time of year and are very defensive of their own nesting sites – this is an instinct that can easily be exploited.

Place a decoy owl or hawk in their territory during the nesting season and corvids will soon rush in to mob it – it's a classic springtime tactic. Get yourself in the right place, and you'll soon learn that crows and magpies aren't always as clever as some people would have you think they are.

The obvious starting point for this sort of hunting is finding a place where crows and/or magpies have set up residence so you can ensure that your decoy is in the right place. The edge of a wood or copse is always a good bet. Look for solitary crows' nests towards the uppermost branches of the loftiest trees – they particularly like a big, sturdy oak or ash. On more open ground, look for the same type of trees growing in hedgerows and you'll probably locate a nest or two. Magpies don't nest so far from the ground and favour thick, overgrown hedgerows with plenty of spiky cover. The large, tangled ball of twigs that constitutes a magpie's nest can often be found deep inside a hedge or spinney of overgrown blackthorn.

I then like to find a fairly open area close to the nest to site my decoy, so it really grabs the attention of passing birds. In my opinion, smaller owl decoys don't stand out enough if they are just plonked on the grass, so it pays to use something like a dead branch or fencepost as a perch and attach

*A decoy little owl can prove irresistible to territorial crows and magpies.*

them with wire or string – this will help it to catch the eye of corvids as they drift by. The bigger owl decoys available from most shooting suppliers can be put straight on the ground, where they'll soon be spotted and investigated. Whichever model you opt for, make sure it is well secured because corvids can get rather boisterous when presented with an unwelcome guest. With bigger decoys, it can pay to jam a sturdy stick into the ground and slide the hollow base over it so they don't fall over if they receive a swipe from an irritated crow.

A great way to add to the impact of your owl decoy is to place a dead magpie at its feet. I've tried placing crow and magpie decoys nearby but, although they help to create the impression of a mobbing in action, they don't create anything like the hysteria that a corpse does. Either hang on to a magpie from a previous hunt (they keep well in the freezer if you share your home with a very understanding person) or wait until you shoot one on the day to make it look like the owl has been caught red-handed. There's no need to be fussy about setting up the dead bird neatly. In fact, you want it to look ruffled – preferably belly-up – as if it's just been bumped off by the offending owl. This scenario will usually (and understandably) get passing corvids rather agitated.

*Decoys with piercing yellow/orange eyes will aggravate corvids the most.*

When choosing your owl decoy, the single most important thing to consider is its eyes. The whole point of using these decoys is to provoke an attack from crows or magpies as they try to defend their nesting territory and, for some reason, they seem to be most aggravated by the imitation owls with the most piercing eyes. Ignore the decoys that have their eyes painted on and go for the ones with staring eyes made from glass or clear, shiny plastic. The best ones have bright yellow eyes with starkly contrasting jet-black pupils.

One of my favourite places to set up such a decoy is in the corner of a field. What I do is set up my decoy owl just out from a likely stretch of hedgerow or woodland edge and then ambush incoming birds from the adjacent hedge, providing there's a safe backstop. Magpies tend to come bouncing along the hedgerow, squawking and clucking at the intruding owl, and fail to notice me lurking on the opposite side of the corner.

We're dealing with sharp-eyed quarry here so a hide is a useful way of keeping out of sight. Don't bother with the tent-style pop-up hides, though, because they'll be spotted and avoided. Opt instead for a discreet net hide, draped in front of your shooting spot and dressed with surrounding weeds, such as ivy and nettle stems, to help it blend in with the background. If you don't have time to construct a convincing hide, it's often better to do without. One thing crows and magpies are very good at is spotting changes in their surroundings and they will notice and shun a hide unless it is very well dressed with vegetation. If it's possible, a natural hide is an even better option that will provide you with an even less conspicuous hiding place. Crawl under the hedgerow, into a ditch or hide yourself among the shrubs or behind a fallen tree and you'll soon disappear from view once you've hidden your human features with a camouflage headnet and gloves.

For best results, it pays to visit the day before you intend to shoot to either establish a natural hide or build your own. This way, you'll cause very little disturbance when you arrive for the

*Weaving a net hide into natural cover is an effective way to keep hidden from sharp-eyed corvids.*

hunt – all you'll have to do is set out your decoy and slip into the cover.

The response to this sort of ambush is usually pretty quick. When corvids spot a bird of prey in their territory they become very agitated and rapidly lose their natural caution. Birds will flight-in, bellowing at the imitation owl as they swoop back and forth. Before long, one will make the mistake of landing in a nearby tree or (if they're feeling particularly brave) pitching on the ground for a closer look. A crow will often open out its large wings and drift down just beyond the decoy to survey it from a seemingly safe distance, but at other times the reaction will be so violent that your imitation owl will be struck by an angry corvid – mine have also had the occasional kicking from passing buzzards!

Magpies tend to arrive in a chattering group, with birds bouncing and flitting in all directions in a black and white blur. Whether your decoy attracts crows or magpies, the noisy reaction of threatened corvids is often so vocal that others will home in to see what all the fuss is about.

The unfolding scene can often be one of complete bedlam with crows and magpies joining the mobbing. Watch the birds and wait until one settles long enough for you to drop it with a shot to the head. As is often the case with corvids, the death of a bird can often provide the hunter with further opportunities as the rest of the clan spiral into a frenzied panic. Rather than doing the sensible thing and flying away from the perceived danger, the remaining birds get even more bold and noisy, and will often land right next to their

*Get the groundwork right and corvids should venture within range of the air rifle.*

fallen comrade. Stay calm and shoot with composure and you should be able to bag a few before the rest eventually wise up and clear off.

Unsurprisingly, the corvids' tendency to mob birds of prey includes the real thing. Therefore, it pays to make yourself ready if you come across an owl, kestrel, buzzard or other raptor when out shooting. Buzzards are very common in my neck of the woods and I've often managed to bag a bonus crow or two by simply keeping still and watching whenever I come across them. Most of the time it'll just be a bunch of crows dive-bombing a buzzard while it soars high overhead; there's no chance of a shot in this instance. Sometimes though, a buzzard or sparrowhawk will swoop into a nearby tree when I'm hunting in the woods. Keep still and quiet and it's surprising how often corvids will turn up to heckle these majestic predators – I've also witnessed grey squirrels having a go. Similarly, shooters should be prepared for crows and magpies to arrive on

the scene if there's a fox around. You'd think they'd have more sense than to attempt to mob such a big animal, but there have been numerous occasions when I've watched crows harassing foxes and I've even seen magpies tweaking their tails.

*A good bag of crows taken using decoy tactics on a spring morning.*

Back to the decoying, as with most things in life, it doesn't always go to plan and there will be days when your plastic owl is flatly ignored. If there is absolutely no response within an hour, it is usually because the trap has been set in the wrong place. This is one advantage of using natural cover instead of a hide because you can travel light and easily move on to target several areas during the same session.

You quickly get a feel for the sort of places that are worth targeting – actually spotting birds is a big indication. Either way, when this method goes to plan it doesn't take long to realise that crows and magpies aren't always as smart as many people think. They aren't stupid, though, and survivors will learn to recognise the decoy and treat it with caution after it's been deployed once or twice on the same ground. When that happens, it's time for a change of tactics.

## The fake nest trick

As I've already mentioned, eggs and chicks are an important part of the spring menu as predators and scavengers strive to build up their own reserves after surviving the perils of winter. Although the nest-robbing habits of corvids make them very unpopular with those of us who like to see wild birds thrive (as well as making them despised by gamekeepers who struggle to protect the vulnerable nests of pheasants and partridges), their inability to leave any nest unmolested can prove to be their own downfall.

By rustling up a simple fake nest to give the impression of a nesting site, the hunter can draw magpies, crows and often jackdaws too, to within range. It is a very useful ruse that I'd overlooked for a while, until I was reminded of its effectiveness during a woodland foray a few years back.

I was spending a fruitless morning in pursuit of squirrels, and couldn't help noticing the exceptional number of magpies that were flitting and squawking along the outer edge of the woods.

The frenzy of nesting activity brought about by a recent spell of warm weather after a long, cold winter was, no doubt, exciting them. The problem was I couldn't get close enough to the black and white bandits to get a shot.

A hasty rummage through my backpack revealed a fresh flask of coffee, some very old cereal bars and other long-forgotten odds and ends, but not the magpie or owl decoy I knew I needed.

While racking my brains for a plan, I remembered that the farmer kept chickens in his garden, so I nipped back to the farmhouse and cajoled a few eggs for my trap. Two hours later I'd accounted for a brace of magpies, and I reckon I'd have had more if I'd had a magpie decoy. That session was a great reminder of just what a draw a fake nest can be, and I've used the method frequently since.

*A simple fake nest can be very effective when scavenging corvids are hunting out a free meal.*

As with using an owl decoy, I don't always go to the trouble of making a proper hide when using a fake nest to draw in crows and magpies. Although you can make good bags from a hide if you put yourself in the right spot, it can pay to stay mobile because these tactics generally only attract corvids that are already in or passing by the immediate area. Sometimes all you need to do is hole-up in the undergrowth, pop off two or three corvids (hopefully), and then move on to another spot. With crows and magpies being so sharp-eyed, it pays to wear full camo and keep your face and hands covered.

Unlike when using the owl decoy, you don't have to find the corvids' nesting site to get the best results from this attractor. You just need a relatively open area so you can set up the nest where passing birds will get a good eyeful of the bait. It usually works best close to the woodland edge or hedgerow that the corvids are patrolling and comfortably within range of wherever you're hiding.

Creating the nest is very simple: I just scrunch up a handful of twigs, dry nettles or cow parsley stems and place them on the ground to form the base. Then, I take a good handful of dry grass and twist it into a ring to create the outer rim of the nest – plonk this onto the base and you'll be amazed at how realistic it looks. For the finishing touch, nestle two or three eggs into your lovingly prepared nest. It's even more irresistible to greedy crows and magpies if you crack one of the eggs to reveal the rich, golden yolk.

Although I didn't have a magpie decoy with me when I resorted to scrounging eggs from the farmer, it can really add to the attraction. The black and white plastic deek will catch the eye of passing birds and draw their attention to your trap. Secondly, the resident corvids will rush towards the nest with even more haste, and with much less caution, if they think an outsider might get there first. Corvids become less cautious when there's a free meal going, but they can become positively reckless if you introduce some competition.

When it comes to selecting crow and magpie decoys, I've yet to be entirely convinced by the flat-pack varieties. On the plus side, these deeks are light and compact to carry and are usually printed in photographic quality with incredibly lifelike plumage. The trouble is, as good as they look when viewed from the side, I can't get past the notion that they must look incredibly one-dimensional from above. By and large, I prefer the bulkier full-bodied decoys and like to ensure that the colourings are bold and eye-catching – especially the white on my magpie decoys. The traditional plastic finish still seems to work as well as ever, although the texture of flock-coated ones does look more realistic. Whatever you go for, try to keep them clean

*One or two decoys will encourage competitive corvids to investigate a fake nest.*

because sharp-eyed corvids don't expect to encounter muddy birds.

A standard plastic magpie decoy usually works perfectly well, but I've been trying something much less subtle over the last couple of seasons, and results have been mixed. Sold to me as The Ultimate Magpie, this curious decoy caught my eye while I was browsing trade stands at a game fair. It's a typical flock-coated magpie deek but it has large foam wings that slot into grooves in its back – it was such an attention grabber that I had to give it a try. The big, outstretched wings give the impression of a magpie flying in to land, and it can be mounted on a springy stick so the occasional puff of wind provides an injection of life and sets it bobbing. While this elaborate decoy certainly doesn't go unnoticed by passing corvids (even when there's no wind to get it moving), birds can sometimes be a little wary of the bizarre-looking creature. It doesn't fail to attract attention from crows and magpies but they sometimes appear to be somewhat intimidated by it, and occasionally refuse to venture too close. It's not a problem if there's a sitty tree nearby, though. Inquisitive birds have often made the mistake of landing in such a tree so they can observe the freaky decoy without having to land near it – I simply pop them off while they're gawping from the branches.

This urge to perch above a potential meal before they commit to landing on the ground can be exploited to make magpies offer clearer shots to the hidden shooter. If there's not a suitable sitty tree for birds to land in and be shot from, I'll sometimes stick a dead branch in the ground to create one. You want a fairly sturdy branch that'll stand three or so feet off the ground and won't fall over if one or two magpies pitch on it. More often than not, incoming magpies will swoop onto your perch to survey from above, rather than plopping straight onto the deck. Presented

*A basic rattle made from a film canister and airgun pellets can be used to mimic the chattering call of a magpie.*

like this, magpies are a lot easier to shoot than when they're hopping about on the ground, and it's also helpful in places where long grass, docks, thistles or nettle stems would otherwise obscure your shots.

I sometimes use a homemade magpie caller to turn heads towards the fake nest. This very basic rattle was made by simply tipping a dozen or so heavy .22 pellets into an old 35mm film canister and then snapping the lid back on. I've tried the

*Set up within range of one or two 'sitty' trees and you should be able to snipe corvids as they survey the scene below.*

*Even with the cover of a hide, a headnet and gloves will improve the hunter's chances of going undetected.*

time-honoured method of rattling a box of matches but it just doesn't make enough noise: the matchbox generates little more than a faint patter, whereas the plastic canister and weighty pellets really do emulate the clack of an agitated magpie.

It's surprising how good this caller is at grabbing the attention of passing magpies, and crows too. I usually give it a few quick rattles and then wait until I hear a bird in the distance. When I get a response, I use the rattle to mimic a chattering call. It's worth easing off with the rattling when the birds get close, though, because it can draw attention to your whereabouts. As I've frequently found, it pays to keep this caller handy – either in your backpack or in a pocket of your shooting jacket – but it's a wise move to tip the pellets out and keep them separate until it's called into action.

Having a rattle in your pocket is a distinct disadvantage when you're hunting on the move.

Incoming corvids can appear literally anywhere when drawn to a fake nest, and the action can become quite frantic. Sometimes the birds hang back and observe the scene from afar, which is why it pays to have an obvious sitty tree within range. This provides edgy crows and magpies with an apparently safe place from which they can inspect the nest of eggs; make sure the tree is within range of your gun and it won't provide them with the sanctuary they expect. On other occasions, especially when you incorporate a decoy, the birds will rush straight in, and you'll find yourself shooting them on the ground. There have been times when I've had to compose shots very quickly to stop them from snaffling back the yolk.

Fortunately, you don't have to rely on the presence of laying hens and the generosity of farmers to furnish your fake nest. I keep hens of my own and pack a couple of eggs when I'm planning to use this method. Alternatively, shop-bought eggs are hardly expensive, so raiding one or two from the fridge at home won't break the bank. If you really want to be prepared for some impromptu corvid control, you could even carry one or two fake eggs along with your film canister. Shops that sell farming supplies tend to sell clay or rubber eggs used by poultry keepers to encourage hens to lay in the right place. I've also seen some

very convincing plastic eggs in toy shops – if you've got children, they've probably got just the thing in their play kitchen. Artificial eggs may lack the alluring yolk of the real thing but at least you'll be ready to capitalise on unexpected opportunities.

## Avoiding April showers

If there's one thing you can count on during a springtime shooting session, it's an unexpected downpour when you really don't want it. Net hides and natural cover don't offer a great deal of protection from the elements, but there is an inexpensive solution to the problem.

Tent-style, pop-up hides are one option but I have never got on particularly well with these. Although such shelters are relatively easy to transport and very quick to assemble, I'm not convinced by their camouflage properties. Most of them are big and boxy, and their bold, straight edges tend to stand out like a beacon unless you go to great lengths to dress them with branches and weeds to make them blend in – and even then they're so much more conspicuous than a net. Above all, pop-up hides don't tend to come cheap, and I don't think they represent particularly good value for money.

However, a cheap fishing umbrella can quickly be converted into a shooting hide and will almost certainly provide better waterproofing than a pop-up hide. Most fishing shops sell economy versions of these big brollies for little more than £20, but you should be able to find something even cheaper at a car boot sale or on the internet.

Open up your fishing umbrella and push the spike into the ground, and you've got protection from the rain

*This magpie tried to scoff the contents of a fake nest and paid the price.*

*Build your hide around a large fishing umbrella and sport can continue regardless of April showers.*

To capitalise on the increased activity, the springtime squirrel shooter has to act fast. The warmth that is causing a frenzy among the animals is also gradually awakening the dormant trees. The sap is beginning to rise, pert green buds are forming and before long there will be a flush of new leaves. The thickening foliage makes it tricky to spot hiding squirrels before they see you approaching and bolt for their dreys or hollowed-out trees, so hit them hard before the canopy closes in.

Most shooters and country people don't need to be reminded of the costly damage that this fluffy little rodent is capable of. Squirrels are omnivorous, which means they'll eat pretty much anything, although tree sap rates very high on their menu through the spring and summer months.

Their lust for tree sap is what makes squirrels so unpopular with foresters. The sharp-toothed rodents strip away swathes of bark from tender young trees so they can lap up the sap as it bleeds down the trunk. In extreme cases, this 'barking' can kill trees, but even minor cases result in deformed specimens with reduced timber value. If there are grey squirrels in the woods where you shoot, take a look at younger trees (especially sappy species like maple) and you'll probably see the gashed scars or dead tops that result from squirrel damage. Squirrels also like to nibble at tender young shoots, which can be equally destructive to growing trees.

wherever you want it. Set it up against a dark backdrop so you aren't silhouetted against light glowing through from the back, and all you have to do is throw a camouflage net over the top and weave in a few weeds to make it disappear into the background.

April showers will never again blight your springtime shooting and, for their price, fishing umbrellas make pretty good frames for net hides whatever the weather. Of course, they really come into their own when there's rain forecast, and you can incorporate them into natural cover to keep you hidden and dry during all kinds of hunting scenarios.

## The roving squirrel shoot

The arrival of spring brings with it a rush of activity among woodland creatures, and that certainly includes grey squirrels. Although these rodents don't hibernate through the winter, as many people mistakenly believe, they certainly venture out more when the temperature begins to rise.

It is no coincidence that this rush of squirrelly activity also coincides with the start of the nesting season. Many people assume that the bushy-tail's diet doesn't extend very far beyond nuts and berries, but the squirrel is a surprisingly aggressive predator. Plant matter forms just a tiny part of the grey squirrel's diet and they'll gladly supplement

surveys have found that their high-protein, nest-robbing binges are having a devastating effect on songbird populations. Ground-nesting game birds also fall prey. As a result of their destructive habits, grey squirrels are despised by foresters and gamekeepers alike. Even so-called nature lovers who have traditionally had a soft spot for the fluffy grey squirrel are beginning to acknowledge the impact its predatory exploits are having on vulnerable wild songbirds.

Their instinctive urge to search out food usually means that squirrels extend their range considerably in the spring, so you can expect to encounter them

*This tree shows the all too common damage caused by bark-stripping squirrels.*

*Early morning is a productive time to drift through the woods in pursuit of squirrels.*

it with something meatier whenever the opportunity presents itself. Nesting season is just getting into full swing and squirrels will already be adding eggs to this season's menu. Later on, when any remaining eggs have hatched, squirrels will use their powerful bark-stripping teeth to tuck into any defenceless young songbirds they encounter on their nest raids.

Grey squirrels are only a relatively recent species to be introduced in the UK and their rapid spread across the country is having a significant impact on native wildlife. Ornithological

virtually anywhere on your woodland shoot. For this reason, I like to stay mobile when targeting grey squirrels in the woods during warmer weather. It enables me to cover a reasonable amount of ground, which will often reveal interesting areas for future investigation – it also helps to keep the gnats and midges at bay. Above all, shooting on the move is a great excuse for taking a stroll in the woods at the time of year when they're at their most beautiful. It's always important to concentrate on the job in hand, but don't forget to soak up your surroundings; the sight of the bluebells and the intoxicating aroma of wild garlic as the tender plants are crushed underfoot. Having permission to experience an unfettered roam through the woods is one of the hunter's greatest privileges, so never take it for granted.

A few words of warning for when you're enjoying the springtime woods: it can be as slippery as hell underfoot. Spring flowers that sprout from bulbs, and bluebells in particular, contain a lush, syrupy slime that can convert the woodland floor into a skating rink when you plant a clumsy boot onto them. I've lost count of the times that I've fallen foul of this devious little trick of nature's: suddenly whizzing along on my heel with the other foot still in the air as I struggle to regain my balance. Most of the time it amounts to little more than an alarming wobble that leaves me charged with adrenaline and thankful that I didn't end up on my backside or with the barrel of my gun stuffed in the ground. It's something well worth being mindful of on flat ground and downright cautious of when scaling steep slopes. It may even spare you the embarrassment of having to own up to spraining your ankle by slipping over on a bluebell!

Camouflage clothing is an asset for the hunter on the move but I don't regard a headnet as essential in this situation because squirrels are not as wary as crows or pigeons. Although a headnet may help to keep biting flies off your face, it will reduce your field of vision and also cause you to overheat when trekking through the woods on warmer days.

One big problem with woodland stalking in the spring is that the ground tends to get rather wet from the April showers. Where you got away with a tough pair of trainers on dry, crisp winter days, you will probably need to wear boots to keep your feet dry now. This makes it a bit harder to creep along, but at least the damp leaves are softer and less crackly, and it's better than squelching around in soggy socks.

When stalking squirrels, I make very slow progress through the woods and stop every five to ten metres to carefully scan the trees above and ahead. Progress is slow because you have to keep shifting your gaze from the treetops to the ground. Scour the woodland floor for any dead twigs, leaves and other debris that may crack under your feet and give away your presence. And remember also to watch the ground ahead for any foraging squirrels – they spend a surprising amount of time on the deck.

*Hunting on the move is a great way to familiarise yourself with your shoot. Promising areas can be earmarked for investigation on future visits.*

*The author steadies his aim as an opportunity arises during a spring morning squirrel shoot.*

The trick is to spot squirrels before they spot you; startled bushy-tails tend to bolt for cover, although they occasionally pause long enough to offer a shot. A good ruse is to locate an oblivious squirrel going about its business and then make maximum use of any available cover or shade to close in until you're within range. Sometimes, it's just a matter of standing still and waiting patiently until an unsuspecting squirrel wanders within range as it scampers among the undergrowth, or scurries from branch to branch among the treetops.

Stationary squirrels can easily go unnoticed, both in the trees and on the ground, so you really have to keep your eyes peeled. Study the woodland carefully every time you pause, and watch out for the tell-tale flick of a bushy tail or a squirrel-shaped outline where branches fork off from the main trunk of a tree. Of course, squirrels are easier to spot when they're on the move: watch for swaying branches and listen for the click of their claws on bark or the rustle of their feet on the woodland floor. Locating squirrels is a knack that improves with experience. As time passes, you'll instinctively learn where to look and how to spot little signs, like the silvery tail poking out from behind a distant bough or the gentle swish of a springing branch.

When a shot presents itself, try to go for the head – it's the most reliable place to cleanly dispatch these robust animals with a sub 12ft.lb air rifle. If the squirrel in your sights is too fidgety for you to hold a steady bead, remember the old trick of pursing your lips and squeaking, or click your tongue in the roof of your mouth. This is usually enough to make a busy squirrel stop and

*It is often possible to flush stubborn squirrels to the gun when hunting with a companion.*

sit up for a look. When Nutkin freezes in a bid to locate the source of the sound, steady your aim and take the shot.

One of the grey squirrel's most notorious and most irritating tricks is to slip around to the back of the tree as you approach it. This can all too easily turn into a hopeless stalemate as your quarry continues to creep round and round the tree as you follow in increasingly futile circles. Thankfully, this trait can easily be turned in your favour if you're shooting with a companion. One of you should stand still and get ready to shoot while the other continues to follow the squirrel around the tree. The man on the move should make no effort to be quiet; in fact, he can be quite noisy as his role is to flush the quarry. All being well, the not-so-clever little bushy-tail will be more concerned about the pursuing 'driver' than the static shooter and will be driven around the tree until it emerges in front of the gun.

If you're presented with a similarly reluctant squirrel when out on your own, you can substitute your mate for a white carrier bag. This ruse doesn't always work but it's certainly worth a try, and I keep a bag in the pocket of my shooting jacket for just such occasions – the bag also comes in handy for sitting on when the ground is wet. What I do when I have a fickle squirrel leading me a merry dance is put on my headnet and gloves and then take out the bag and spread it open on the woodland floor. I then continue to stalk the squirrel around the tree: very slowly and very quietly. If the plan works, the squirrel will be more alarmed by the sight of the unnaturally bright white bag than by my approach, and will stop and stare at the intrusive object while I creep round and take a shot.

Incidentally, the aforementioned ruse of herding a squirrel around a tree with the help of a companion is an important reminder of the way quarry can be flushed by all kinds of disturbances in the woods. Walkers and horse riders are very likely to drive birds and mammals ahead of them and, while your first reaction to somebody else's presence should always be to ensure that there's no chance of a shot travelling in their direction, your second one should be to expect spooked critters to be running or flying ahead of them. An extreme example of this is the arrival of the gamekeeper on his quad bike on one of my shooting permissions. On a still day, I can hear the quad bike coming from literally miles away – and so can all of the creatures that live in the woods. When I hear the rasp of the engine approaching across the fields, I take it as a cue to keep very still and very quiet. From a makeshift hiding place behind a tree or against a bank, I often see first deer and then sometimes a fox or two trotting past as they dash ahead of the approaching keeper. Squirrels, magpies and jays also shift through the trees as the noise gets nearer, and I frequently get shots by simply being ready after being alerted by the distant sound.

*Squirrels can be difficult to spot in the treetops, so take your time and look very carefully.*

*A brace of squirrels bagged during a rove through the woods.*

Sometimes, as you make your way through the woods, you'll encounter an area that warrants closer attention. Perhaps a pair of squirrels made a dash for cover as you approached, maybe you've encountered what looks like an active drey, or do you just have the feeling that the tangle of ivy draped around a big, old oak is hiding a squirrel or two? Find such a place and it's often worth sitting quietly and waiting in case squirrels venture out when peace returns to the woods. Linger until a shot presents itself, or you grow tired of waiting and then drift on in search of another opportunity.

Working the woods in this way is a productive and enjoyable way to round off the peak squirrel season before dense summer foliage makes controlling these artful little rodents a very tricky business. And don't just expect to encounter squirrels; move quietly and pigeons and crows are also likely to feature in the bag.

One thing that can hamper the roving squirrel shooter's progress is the burden of carrying shot quarry – and you don't always want to be lumbered with a backpack or game bag. The trouble is, their smooth fur makes squirrels difficult to grip and they aren't particularly light, especially when you're trying the carry three or four. I always keep a few lengths of string (or more often bailer twine) in a pocket of my hunting jacket, and this can be used to fashion a simple game carrier that will stop squirrels from slipping out of your hands. All I do is tie a loop in one end of the string to create a handle and then lash my shot squirrels tightly to the other end. It's a very basic solution but it does the trick.

I think it's fair to assume that most people hunt squirrels for pest control purposes rather than for the pot. That said, more and more people are starting to regard them as meat for the table and I now get regular requests from farm shops and butchers whose customers have developed a taste for this wild fare.

Whatever your view on the culinary qualities of grey squirrels, it is a pity to waste them. If you don't fancy eating them, try to find an outlet for the meat: apart from butchers and restaurants, people who keep ferrets should be grateful, as will people who keep birds of prey. And remember that merchants who trade in tying materials for fly fishing hooks will pay a few quid for a decent bundle of squirrels' tails; you should be able to find contact details for them on the internet. There's no harm in making the most of a successful pest control foray, and it certainly provides another incentive to get out there.

# Garden pest control

If I have to call on my airgun for garden pest control it's usually in the spring, and it's usually because I can't stop woodpigeons from pulling up my onion sets!

In the hunting field, the limited power of air rifles can sometimes feel like a disadvantage because we have to get close to our quarry to ensure clean, humane kills. But in the garden, the comparatively low power and near-silent operation of airguns is a massive advantage. Lower power means you can easily determine where your shots terminate, and the muted muzzle report of a silenced airgun is unlikely to cause irritation to neighbours.

I'm a little more tolerant of airgun quarry species in my garden than I am on my shoots. I like to encourage all sorts of wildlife in the garden but there are times when pests conflict with my own interests, or start to impact on populations of more vulnerable species, and action needs to be taken. My garden pest control rounds have included rabbits nibbling at the vegetable patch, rats around the chicken run and compost bins, crows and magpies raiding the nests of resident songbirds and grey squirrels trashing nut feeders put out for the birds.

Prevention is better than cure, so I always try to ensure that measures are in place to stop pests from making a nuisance of themselves. The fine wire mesh around my chicken run is buried a foot under the ground so rats are discouraged from burrowing under to help themselves to the poultry feed. Also, I keep a Fenn trap permanently set in a wooden tunnel on the boundary of the chicken run, so I soon find out when the scaly-tails are patrolling.

But, during the spring, my regular morning stroll around the garden to check plants and pets will occasionally reveal some unwanted visitors to the vegetable patch. On one occasion last year, I was horrified to discover that around 50 onion sets (approximately half of my crop) had been picked out and eaten in one hit. Rather than letting

*The limited power of airguns is an advantage in the garden, where guns with more grunt are simply too dangerous to use.*

rip at the offending woodpigeons, I decided to replant the gaps and adopt preventative measures by propping a net over the vegetable patch.

The next morning, when I peeped out of the window to glance at my crops, I was shocked and enraged to see a woodpigeon under the net, helping itself to the replenished rows of onions. I ran out of the house and the startled woodpigeon flapped out from beneath the net and settled in a nearby apple tree, to watch me fix the netting back down.

With the crop apparently secured, I went back into the house and, ten minutes later, was even more infuriated to see that the bird had somehow managed to get itself under the net and was once more tucking into my onions. It appeared that, although the net had discouraged most of the local woodies, this cocky individual was determined to get at what was growing beneath.

I was now content that this pigeon's actions satisfied the requirements of the General Licence that governs the control of specified avian pests; protection and scaring had failed to discourage the bird from damaging my crop and it was making a serious nuisance of itself. I was keen to remedy the situation but, however tempting it was to pop the pigeon straight off its favourite perch in the apple tree, I needed to adopt a far more responsible approach.

Shooting airguns in the garden is quite acceptable, but you're breaking the law the moment a pellet strays beyond your boundary. For this reason, a shot up into a tree is just too risky. Likewise, the wooden panel fence behind my vegetable patch is completely inadequate as a backstop.

The best means of stopping pellets in the garden is a wall of brick or stone, but a large patio slab is a handy, portable alternative that can be set up just where you need it. An upright concrete slab stops pellets as effectively as a wall, preventing any risk of ricochet, but don't be tempted to use a wooden board instead. Even if the wood is robust enough to stop the pellet from ripping through it, its fibrous nature means it could bounce it back at an alarming speed. The risk of unpredictable ricochets therefore means that wood should not be used as a backstop.

When targeting the onion-munching woodie, I propped the slab against the edge of the vegetable patch and placed a handful of poultry grain in front of it, in the hope of luring the pigeon into position before it made for my veggies. Most gardens offer plenty of hiding places: I hid in the shed to wait for this woodie, but I've snuck behind shrubs and compost bins and even under patio furniture when controlling pests in the garden.

The cocky woodpigeon fell for my trap and his crop-gobbling days were swiftly ended, but this technique can be utilised to control more than just pigeons. I've placed my concrete slab backstop behind rat-runs and piled chicken feed and even tinned sweetcorn in front to safely dispatch rats; I've put it in front of compost heaps and baited it with vegetable scraps to take out scavenging rats, crows and magpies; and I've set it up at the base of the bird table and used heaps of peanuts as bait when faced with marauding grey squirrels.

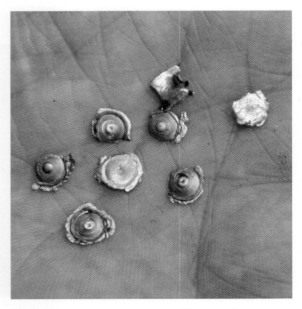

*These airgun pellets were safely obliterated by a concrete backstop.*

When it comes to ridding gardens of rabbits that have been munching vegetables or scraping holes into finely kept lawns, the slab backstop doesn't really work because bunnies never tend to emerge where you want them to. Unless you're shooting in a walled garden or where there's a decent bank to keep shots safely contained, the best option is to get yourself into an elevated position. From here you'll be shooting at a downward angle and the pellet's flight-path will terminate harmlessly when it wallops into the ground.

# Down on the farm

Much of my springtime pest control takes place around farmyards and, just like in the garden, the limited power of the air rifle is a real boon when shooting in the vicinity of farm buildings.

At this time of year, avian species are likely to be causing problems. The rats that were drawn in by the lure of food and shelter during the winter will be dispersing back into the countryside now that natural food sources are again becoming abundant, but they're often replaced by nesting birds.

It's not unusual for me to spend hours of my time controlling magpies and crows around the woods and hedgerows, only to be reminded by the farmer that other species are causing problems closer to home. While I've been out in the countryside, pest species like collared doves, feral pigeons and even jackdaws will often have moved into the farm units in search of nesting sites. Large, shady barns with a skeleton of old wooden beams in the roof space, and even modern units with criss-crossing steel joists, provide places for these birds to nest where they can keep watch for danger from these high man-made perches. Feral pigeons in particular do well in this environment (especially if there's a handy supply of feed to keep them nourished) and their populations can often reach epidemic proportions. When large flocks get a hold, farmers are faced not only with the problem of considerable amounts of valuable foodstuff being consumed by unwanted guests, but also with the hygiene threat posed by their droppings. It's bad enough having pests fouling the water and feed troughs of farm animals, but the risks posed by hundreds of disease-spreading birds crapping over stores of food produced for human consumption is far worse.

Feral pigeons are descendants of the true rock dove, which is protected. These birds have the same Latin name (Columba livia) and were domesticated and bred for food in the Middle Ages. Nowadays, feral pigeons are found around farm units and warehouses. They're not just a problem in rural areas but also cause considerable problems with fouling inside and outside derelict buildings around towns and cities. Unregulated populations of feral pigeons can become very large, making them far more prone to disease than woodpigeons and collared doves. Many people refer to them as flying rats, and they certainly aren't fit for the table. Collared doves, however, are cleaner living and make good eating; their meat is much the same as woodpigeon, you just need more of it because they're smaller birds.

You'll see feral pigeons of all colours and mixes of colours, including grey, white, brown and black, with patches of buff pink and metallic green thrown in for good measure. They're quite easy to distinguish from wild species of pigeon and dove, but the hunter must be very careful not to confuse 'ferals' with racing pigeons, which come in a similar variety of colours. Disorientated racers do crop up on farms from time to time and, by and large, tend to look fitter and more alert than feral pigeons. The best way to distinguish between them is the telltale ring on the leg of a racing pigeon. Pigeon-fanciers can grow very attached to their birds, which are sometimes worth several hundreds of pounds, and shooting one is tantamount to killing somebody's pet. Check carefully through your scope to see if there's a ring before you shoot. If you're anything but certain, don't pull the trigger.

*Picking off avian pests as they swoop in to raid the maize silage.*

Approach farmers sensibly, and it shouldn't be difficult to secure a bit of farmyard pest control. You are, after all, doing them a favour. In fact, potting vermin around farm buildings has given many shooters their first taste of air rifle hunting – myself included. The abundance of quarry, and easy ambush opportunities around barns and outbuildings means it can be much easier for less experienced shooters to get close enough for a shot, certainly compared with stalking over open fields or waiting in the woods. However, despite the seemingly straightforward opportunities they offer, farmyards probably present the air rifle hunter with more potential hazards than any other scenario, so it's critical to ensure a safe shooting routine.

First and foremost, farms are a place of work; apart from causing a terrible injury, or even death, an accident could be ruinous to a whole family's livelihood. Whenever you plan to shoot around farm buildings, ensure that you know who is working and exactly where, then let them know of your intentions before you start. Spring is usually a particularly busy time on the farm: the growing season is getting underway and farmers will be wanting to make the most of the lengthening days. You may have to adjust your plans to accommodate farming operations, but it's always better to be safe than sorry.

Of course, other than human safety, there is often the welfare of livestock to consider. Always ensure that there's no chance of a miss or a ricochet harming farm stock before you pull the trigger. One of the best ways to ensure that you don't pose a danger to animals is to situate yourself close to them, that way you'll always know exactly where they are. If there's a pen of calves at one end of a barn I'm targeting, I'll usually set up with my back to their enclosure so I know they'll be safe from my shots. Don't forget to keep yourself safe, too; it can pay to keep close to livestock but not too close. Most people would have the sense to keep clear of a bull, but there's a real danger of getting crushed by a herd of frisky young cattle or kicked by a flighty horse, especially if you're in a confined space. Exercise caution and common sense at all times.

The fabric of buildings and machinery must also be considered, otherwise you could face the embarrassment of a costly repair bill and certain banishment from the farm, and all the other farms and estates in your locality once word gets around. News travels fast in rural communities – and bad news travels fastest of all.

Modern farm machinery can cost tens of thousands of pounds, so think twice about the likely outcome before taking a shot at the feral pigeon pecking at grain in front of a parked tractor. Fortunately, there's a lot of concrete around farmyards; it's a great backstop material that obliterates airgun pellets. But have your wits about you if you're targeting collared doves or feral pigeons in the rafters; you'll soon get the boot (and the bill) if stray shots result in a leaky roof. I often shoot with high-powered, FAC-rated air rifles, but never around farm buildings. This type of shooting is usually done at close quarters so the extra grunt of FAC power is not necessary and would only increase the risk of an accident.

All shooters should have insurance, wherever they hunt, but it's imperative if you shoot around farm buildings. A reasonably inexpensive (certainly inexpensive compared with the money you paid for your shooting gear) premium will buy you suitable cover, but don't just go for the cheapest deal. As with most things, you get what you pay for, and a reputable company is likely to give you the best service if you ever have to put them to the test. If you take your shooting seriously, which you should, I would recommend joining the British Association for Shooting and Conservation (BASC). This organisation works hard to protect the future of shooting and membership includes comprehensive insurance. Essential as insurance is, it's your job as a responsible shooter to take measures to ensure that you never need to call on it.

Eradicating feral pigeons is pretty straightforward. They aren't as wary as their wild cousins so it's usually just a case of walking around the barns and nailing as many as possible before they spook. Because you're hunting at close range and need to get shots off quickly, open sights can actually perform better than telescopic sights in this situation. Target acquisition is faster when using 'opens' because your eye doesn't have to get accustomed to the optics. Also, .22 calibre is generally favoured because it delivers more of a clout than the zippy .177, which can sometimes drill straight through without delivering sufficient shock to the vital organs to cause an instant kill. When hunting at under 20 metres, a strike to the heart and lung area should be sufficient to achieve clean kills when using a relatively hefty pellet. For this reason, dedicated farmyard pest controllers often opt for .25 calibre. This beast of a pellet has a trajectory that I regard as being just too curvy to be used for hunting at mid- to long-range in the open field, but it's absolutely devastating at close range.

By and large, pest species aren't as suspicious around farmyards as they are on open countryside, because they are used to frequent disturbance by workers and machinery. As previously mentioned, feral pigeons can be downright stupid, but collared doves, jackdaws and the occasional woodpigeon, magpie and crow will usually prove to be a little more artful. You'll need to keep hidden from sight, but camouflage isn't as important as it is in the woods; there's no need to go dressed as a tree, and a headnet certainly isn't essential. Rather than the usual green attire, I try to wear muted greys and browns that will blend in with the farmyard surroundings. Being right-handed, I do my best to move around the outside of buildings in an anticlockwise direction when stalking. This means that my gun comes to shoulder on the outside if I happen to spot some quarry as I peep around the corner. This very simple trick makes shooting a lot easier and saves you from having to move outwards, and into view, when shooting around an obstacle that you're using for cover. If you're left-handed simply reverse the technique by moving around in a clockwise direction.

Conveniently, farmyards are usually cluttered with things that make for good hiding places. Straw bales, piles of fertiliser sacks, discarded pallets and the like can often be utilised as makeshift hides. You might even be able to take advantage of an outbuilding that provides you with a discreet shooting place, or even a shady corner within a large barn. It's not difficult to find dark, shady places around the farmyard and that's often all the cover you'll need. These ready-made hiding places are some of the best a hunter can use because there's no need to change the existing arrangement; incoming birds will find the place exactly as they left it and will therefore have no cause for concern.

When culling feral pigeons, it's usually a case of taking them as you find them, but I tend to give a little more thought when targeting other avian pests on the farm. I usually begin by working out what's attracting them – it could be a food source or an inviting nesting site – and then think about how best to ambush them when they return. Very often, incoming birds will stop to survey the farmyard from a high perch before continuing into the buildings, and these lookout posts can be a great place to target them. Places worth considering include grain silos and tall trees growing on the edge of the farmyard. Set yourself up in a hidden spot from where you can cover one of these perches and you should be able to determine the range you'll be shooting at and ensure that all shots are taken at a safe angle well

*A brace of collared doves shot around farm buildings. Vast flocks of these birds can cause serious problems if left unchecked.*

away from workers, livestock and machinery. Take time to make yourself comfortable; think about your shooting position and ways in which you can improve stability when shots arise (perhaps you can move a hay bale or a couple of pallets to create a steady rest for your gun). Simple preparations like this will enable you to snipe with deadly accuracy when avian pests drop in.

As well as determining where incoming birds are likely to land, it's also sensible to work out where they're likely to fall when you shoot them. It's important to make sure that all shot quarry can be easily recovered so it can either be taken home for the pot or properly disposed of on the farm. Farmers don't want to find their premises littered with bodies after your visit and many will not tolerate such slobbish behaviour.

# The traditional May rook shoot

May 12th used to be a big day in the countryside calendar. It was, and in some rural communities still is, the date of the customary 'brancher' shoot. Brancher is the name given to fledgling rooks when they venture from their nests in towering treetops to take clumsy steps onto precarious branches in preparation for their first flight. This treetop spectacle takes place around the same few days in May each year and, no thanks to the culinary reputation of rook pie, many of the participants never make it to their maiden flight.

Brancher shooting was once so popular that men and women of all ages would join in with the proceedings, and some exquisite little guns were crafted especially for the job. From mini-shotguns to dainty little rifles, countless weapons were tailor-made just for the big occasion that was the annual rook shoot. Some of them are still around today, and those that have been properly looked after fetch a decent sum when they go under the auctioneer's hammer.

The tender breast meat of a young rook is supposed to be a real delicacy, but I'm afraid I just can't bring myself to even consider eating any member of the corvid family. Once you've seen these birds scavenging around waste tips and snaffling back putrid chunks of decaying road-kill, it's difficult to get excited at the prospect of tucking into one.

Whether or not you fancy a meal of rook pie, the May brancher days are the best time for reducing the size of a burgeoning rookery. The naïve young birds aren't at all wary of people and aren't very mobile, so they're easy work for the air rifle hunter who understands the performance of his gun when shooting at a steep upward angle. And make sure you do, because young rooks deserve the same respect and swift dispatch afforded to all other quarry species.

It's easy to assume that a pellet flying straight up into the air would strike lower than usual as it is faced with more resistance from gravity, but that's not always the case. When we zero our sights while shooting flat, gravity is pulling down against the near-horizontal path of the pellet. Because the pellet emerges from the barrel below the line of sight, it rises up to the primary point of zero somewhere around 15 metres and then continues to rise just above the line of sight before gravity drags it back down to the secondary zero at around 25 metres.

However, when you fire directly upwards, gravity is pulling straight back on the pellet from behind. As a result, the pellet will still cross the line of sight somewhere around the primary zero but, without gravity pulling along the length of the flight path, it won't be pulled back to the secondary zero. The consequence will be a miss above the target, or more specifically behind you if you're shooting straight up, so you'll need to aim low (use hold-under) when making this type of shot.

However, if you relax the upward angle – shooting towards the top of a tree from a few metres to the side, for instance – the effect of gravity will drag the pellet back down after it rises above the primary zero. Of course, there are further variations between this angle and upwards to vertical, and back down to horizontal, but this basic theory should set you on the right track. You'll need to master it in practice before you tackle live quarry and the only way to achieve that is to set up targets at various angles and see for yourself where shots land and where you need to aim to bring them back on target. Dead branches, the soft decaying ones that pose no risk of ricochet, are handy marks for this type of practice as are acorns and conkers later in the year.

Getting back on track, rooks aren't such aggressive predators as crows and magpies, and they can actually do some good by feeding on creepy-crawly pests such as wireworms (the larvae of a beetle which munches holes in the roots of crops) and leather jackets (daddy-long-legs larvae which live in the top layer of soil and eat grass roots). Nonetheless, their place on Natural

*Expect to be presented with some high shots when thinning out 'brancher' rooks.*

England's General Licence is quite justified. A sizeable flock (the collective noun is a parliament) of rooks can do major damage to agricultural crops. These birds have a habit of using their long beak to pick freshly drilled seeds from the ground – a trait that makes them less than popular with many farmers. I've also been called in to control rooks when they've descended on the farmyard en masse to scavenge animal feed. Numbers also sometimes need to be controlled when oversized rookeries close to homes begin to create the combined nuisance of noise from relentlessly cawing birds and filth from the constant patter of droppings.

Rooks are sociable birds that don't mind living cheek to jowl, and populations can sometimes spiral out of control. Brancher season is a good time to thin them out when this is the case, but think twice if a complete eradication is requested. To me, the rookery is a quintessential part of rural England, and our villages would be all the poorer without them.

Adult rooks can also be shot from a hide when they are devouring seed drillings on the open field, or from the cover of farm buildings when they're scavenging food. A couple of crow decoys set out on freshly ploughed or drilled land is usually enough to draw them within range. But don't expect fully-grown rooks to be anything like as gullible as branchers. These birds are intelligent, fast-learning corvids that share the crow's cunning and its fear of man. You'll have to keep well hidden if you want to get close enough for a shot.

In terms of its appearance, the rook is fairly similar to the carrion crow. They're about the same size, but there is a reliable way of distinguishing between the two. Whereas the head and beak of the crow is entirely black, the rook has a white mask around the base of the beak, nostrils and chin. The beak is also slightly longer and more pointed than that of the crow. The rook's plumage also looks scruffy compared with the crow's, especially around the thigh feathers, which are often described as looking like a pair of baggy trousers, and the croaking waak-waak call of the rook is nothing like as shrill as the shriek of the crow.

# Recipes for spring

### SQUIRREL SURPRISE

I'm not the world's greatest fan of squirrel meat, but there are lots of people who love the stuff and it is a pity not to make use of food harvested in the field. This is a variation of a recipe that was passed on by a friend who found it on the internet. Search around and you'll find hundreds, probably thousands, of recipes for game on the web.

I have to concede that this dish is actually pretty good, either served on rice or with a dollop of mashed potato, and the slow cooking certainly makes the squirrel meat tender. When my mate serves it, he adds what he believes to be a hilarious twist (though the jury is still out on that one) by leading his guests to believe they're eating chicken until they've finished wolfing it down, at which points he tells them it was squirrel. That's the surprise!

If you can't lay your hands on any squirrel meat, simply swap for one decent-sized rabbit.

*To serve 2*

**Ingredients**
Best meat from 2 grey squirrels, deboned and cut into chunks.
Knob of butter
3 rashers of smoked bacon
1 large onion, chopped
1 can of cream of chicken soup
570ml of water
3 heaped tablespoons of peanut butter (squirrels and nuts are a classic combination)
3 medium carrots, chopped
150g of green beans (fresh or frozen), halved
225g mushrooms, sliced
2 sprigs of fresh rosemary, finely chopped
Salt and pepper

Preheat the oven to 180°C and melt the butter in a casserole dish on the hob. Cut the bacon into 2cm pieces and add, along with the chunks of squirrel meat. Cook, stirring occasionally, until the meat begins to brown, then add the onion and cook until it begins to soften. Stir in the peanut butter and remove from the heat.

Add the carrots and mushrooms along with the green beans, then pour in the soup and water. Add the finely chopped rosemary and season with salt and pepper. Give the mixture a good stir, cover and place in the preheated oven for 1 hour. Remove and stir, then return to the oven for a further 30 minutes before serving.

## ROOK PIE

Although I've never felt particularly inclined to eat any member of the corvid family, rook pie is a classic country dish, so I felt it was only right to include the recipe.

This version was passed on by a friend and should be just the thing if you feel like getting busy in the kitchen after a successful morning thinning out the branchers. And remember, it's those tender young branchers you want, because the breast meat from older rooks is bitter and far less palatable.

If you don't fancy trying rook, you can always use the breast meat from 3 or 4 woodpigeons instead. In fact, if you swap the rook for pigeon and substitute the stewing steak for a rabbit, you should have the makings of a thoroughly tasty game pie.

*To serve 4*

### Ingredients

1 packet (225g) of shortcrust pastry (or see Pigeon Pasties recipe on page 94 to make your own)
Breast meat from 6 brancher rooks, cut into chunks
450g stewing steak, cut into chunks
225g mushrooms, sliced
55g plain flour
Large knob of butter
1 medium onion, chopped
2 glasses of dry white wine
285ml of strong beef stock
Herbs of your choice
1 egg

Preheat the oven to 180°C. Dice the rook breasts and steak into rough chunks, then place into a bowl and roll in the flour until covered. Chop the onion and slice the mushrooms. Melt the butter in a large frying pan, add the onion and fry until it begins to soften. Add the meat and fry until lightly browned, and then add the sliced mushrooms and fry for another 2 minutes. Pour in 2 glasses of white wine and stir to deglaze the pan. Sprinkle in the chopped herbs, add the stock and stir until it begins to thicken. Season to taste and the pie filling is finished.

Grease a 25cm pastry dish with butter. Roll out the pastry on a lightly floured work surface and line the dish – keep the remaining pastry and roll it out for the pie lid. Pour the meat mixture into the pastry-lined dish, brush the top of the pastry with the beaten egg and place the pastry lid on top. Crimp down the edges and make 3 or 4 slices in the lid to stop it from splitting. Brush top with egg and place in the oven for 40 minutes or until golden-brown.

Serve with parsnip purée and peas.

## PIGEON ROLLS

Woodpigeon is the fullest-flavoured meat to grace the airgun shooter's table. In fact, some people find it tastes a little too meaty – especially when served on its own as a classic pan-fried dish.

But there's no reason for anyone to miss out on this delicious meat and, fortunately, there are plenty of ways to mute the robust flavour of pigeon.

My very easy-to-make pigeon rolls are perfect for picnics, so rustle up a batch for the hamper, or slip them into your backpack if you want a wholesome bite when you're out with the gun.

The addition of sausage meat to the pigeon breast mellows the flavour considerably, and everyone who's tried them has wolfed these savoury pastries down. My children, who don't think they like pigeon, absolutely love these 'sausage rolls' and they're now a regular item in their lunchboxes. So try this twist on sausage rolls for a melt-in-the-mouth pastry snack that should appeal to all palates – even those who don't think they like game.

*Makes 4*

### Ingredients

1 packet of ready-made puff pastry (500g)
Breast meat from 2 woodpigeons, finely diced
3 large pork sausages, skinned
Herbs (fresh or dried)
1 egg
1 handful of plain flour
Knob of butter
Salt and pepper

Preheat the oven to 180°C. Start by removing the skin from the sausages – discard the membrane and place the meat in a mixing bowl. Finely dice the pigeon breasts and add to the sausage meat. Chop herbs of your choice (I favour sage and rosemary, but wild garlic is also great if it grows in the woods where you shoot) and add to the bowl along with a good twist of salt and pepper. Roll up your sleeves and thoroughly mix the ingredients into a meaty ball.

Cover the work surface with a dusting of plain flour to stop the pastry from sticking. Ready-made puff pastry usually comes in 500g blocks – you'll need about half. Roll out the pastry lengthways until around 3mm thick, then cut the sheet in two. You should have 2 squares of roughly 30cm by 20cm.

Split the meatball in two and use your hands to roll it into sausages to fit the length of your pastry pieces. Place the meat on the pastry and roll it up. Stick the join where the pastry meets with some beaten egg and ensure that it's at the bottom of the roll so it doesn't split open during cooking.

Cut off any excess pastry and slice each of your rolls in two – you should end up with 4 of around 15cm each. Place on a baking tray that has been greased with butter, lightly score the tops and glaze the pastry with the egg wash. Place in the oven and cook for 25 minutes or until golden-brown.

# SUMMER

*High summer usually brings with it some of the finest pigeon and
rabbit shooting of the year. Sun-ripened cornfields are a favourite of the woodpigeon,
and rabbits, including plenty of gullible young'uns, will be enjoying
the sweet sugar-rich grass growing in the pastures.*

*Despite the glut of quarry species, summer can prove tricky for the
air rifle hunter because wild creatures keep strange hours when the days are long and hot.
Dawn and dusk are the prime times, with many long unproductive
hours between them. You'll be kept from your bed, but expect to be rewarded with the
chance to savour glorious misty sunrises when the rest of the world is still asleep
and hazy red sunsets when they're slipping back under their blankets.*

# Stalking rabbits

Summer is one of the best times for hunting rabbits. A couple of months have passed since the peak breeding season of spring and lots of young rabbits are nibbling their way through the grassland. As a result, there should be plenty of farmers who would appreciate some help in keeping their numbers down. What's more, rabbits taste fantastic at this time of year: the three-quarter grown 'harvest' bunnies have spent their short lives fattening-up on sweet sugary grass, and their flesh is incredibly tender compared with that of older rabbits, which have overwintered.

One of my favourite ways of hunting rabbits at this time of year is to stalk them. Hunting on the move is challenging stuff because quarry is adept at detecting movement. But that added element of difficulty is what makes a successful stalk all the more satisfying; you've pitted your wits against the finely-tuned defence mechanisms of a wild creature, and won. Furthermore, a roving approach is a good excuse for spending a peaceful summer's evening strolling around the meadows.

Stalking is as close as air rifle hunting gets to a head-to-head; it's you against your quarry and the tension can reach fever pitch as you inch closer and closer to that decisive moment. The difficult thing is deciding when that moment should be. Do you seize the first opportunity and go for a long-range shot that carries a considerable risk of missing (or worse still, wounding), or push your luck and hope that the bunny doesn't clock you and bolt as you sneak even closer to set up an easier shot?

As the name implies, stalking is about creeping within range of your mark. The problem is that rabbits are programmed with a survival instinct that helps them dodge foxes, buzzards and stoats on a daily basis, so they aren't just going to sit there while you or I try to stroll up and pop them off.

Stealth is the first and last word in stalking and it begins before you leave the house. Rabbits have ears like radars so you have to think very carefully about your choice of clothing. Your stalking outfit

*Stalking is one of the most challenging and gratifying ways to hunt rabbits during the summer.*

*Stalking can be very effective when rabbits venture out to feed at dusk.*

should be as near silent as possible, so you need to avoid or remedy clinking zips and rattling buckles before you set off.

Footwear also needs to be right for the job. Sometimes, wet weather will force you to wear wellies, but these are far from ideal, and so are heavy, clumpy boots that, in spite of the wonderful support they provide, don't allow you to flex your ankle properly or feel the ground through their soles. In my experience, the best footwear to wear when stalking rabbits is a lightweight pair of hiking-style trainers. And don't replace them too quickly because, like a good wine, they tend to improve with age. They may look tatty, but an aging pair of shoes is a supple pair of shoes, and they'll help you to make the light, soft footfalls that are necessary when stalking.

As well as very good hearing, and a frustratingly good ability to detect vibrations through the ground, rabbits also have a highly evolved sense of smell and they can detect the whiff of a human from a massive distance. Strong aftershave will have the rabbits dashing for cover before you get anywhere near them and so will the smell of washing powder on your clothes. Of course, hunting clothes need to be cleaned from time to time, but I just wash mine in clean water to minimise unnatural fragrances. The smell of cigarettes is another alien odour, which will be treated with suspicion, so don't go out stinking of fags if you want to get close to the bunnies.

Out in the field, the wind direction will help you to make a very important decision before you set off. Ideally, you want whatever breeze there is to be blowing in your face. This will help to waft the danger signal of human smells away from your quarry and, however hard you try, you'll always be carrying a certain amount of odour, from your body, from your car and from the places you frequent during the day. Stalking into the wind will also help to ensure that unavoidable sounds are swept away from your quarry rather than towards it.

You probably won't be able to get around your entire shoot with the wind in your face, but I do my best to make sure that I'm downwind of my quarry as I approach the areas I expect to produce the most action.

Rabbits are largely nocturnal and usually venture out furthest from cover at night. Therefore, dusk and dawn are the best times to target them, at either end of their night-time binge. Ironically, these are the quietest times of the day in terms of ambient noise, so you have to go into stealth mode from the start. Think of all the things that could make rabbits edgy – like slamming car doors – and try to avoid them.

Gateways are a nightmare for the hunter on the move, as they can seldom be negotiated without making a noise. The tinny 'clank' of the tripping latch on a traditional five-bar gate cuts through the still evening air like a knife, and it's probably fair to assume that rabbits learn to listen out for it. Some gates open and close more quietly than others, while climbing will sometimes be the least noisy option. I'm afraid that knowing which method to apply when is a matter of trial and error, so it's a question of familiarising yourself with your shoot and working out how best to cross each gate. If you do decide to climb, do it slowly and stay as close to the hinged end as you possibly can – there's more support at this end so the gate is less inclined to bounce and clang as you shift your weight.

Gates do have their advantages, though, and frequently provide the roving hunter with the chance of an easy shot. Gateways create a 'window' through to the opposite side of the hedgerow you are walking along, so always approach them slowly and quietly, then peep through and have a thorough look at what's on the other side before you pass by or climb over. You'll be surprised how many times you'll spot a rabbit or two grazing contentedly on the other side, and within range of your gun. In this case,

the gate will often serve one final function as a handy gun rest as you compose your shot.

It's not just noisy gates that can put the mockers on a stalking session: walkers, and dog walkers in particular can really mess things up. Like it or not, as long as they stick to public footpaths, walkers have every right to enjoy the countryside, but they do tend to put the rabbits on edge. If the roamers have a dog with them, and especially if they're ignorant enough to let their pet run off the lead, then you can be assured that the resident bunnies will be seriously alarmed and it'll be some time before they pluck up the courage to venture back out. If I encounter dog walkers when I'm out stalking, I try to adjust my route to give them the widest possible clearance.

Clearly, a cautious approach is the key to catching your quarry unawares, but when you do spot rabbits you can expect to have to crank the stealth up by several more gears if you want to succeed.

Once I have spotted my quarry, I freeze and don't move until I have fully analysed the situation. Before I move on I want to establish several things: the wind direction, the place I need to reach to take the shot, any cover I can exploit to get me there and anything that is likely to blow my cover. I have lost count of the number of times unseen pigeons have burst out of an overhead tree and sent the rabbits bolting for cover. Blackbirds are another hazard the stalker has to watch out for. If you spot one ahead, wait until it passes rather than risk spooking it and sending it into a squawking rage. The shrill alarm call of the blackbird is recognised by most wild creatures as a sign of imminent danger and is guaranteed to put everything on edge.

If I'm carrying a laser rangefinder, I'll give it a quick 'zap' to see how far away the rabbits are. In normal conditions, I'd want to get myself to within 30 metres to take the shot, closer if obstacles such as tall nettles or thistles force me to take a standing shot – a notoriously unstable stance. Assuming, for the sake of argument, the rabbit or rabbits I have seen turn out to be 120

*The author ranges a group of rabbits as he plans his stalking route.*

metres away, I then use the rangefinder again and mentally mark the spot to which I need to travel in order to be 90 metres towards them – I then know that I'll be 30 metres away from my mark when I reach this place. Often, I'll not be carrying my rangefinder so I'll estimate range as I advance and decide on my shooting position as I get closer.

Next, I'll be looking for whatever cover I can utilise to hide my approach. An overhanging hedgerow, any dark areas of shade, patches of vegetation and humps and bumps in the ground are all natural features that can be exploited to keep you out of sight. Once I have a plan in mind, I proceed – but very gingerly. Footsteps are slow and light and I try to 'read' the ground with my feet, because a cracking twig would be disastrous at this stage.

It's important to stay as low as you can and keep as tight as possible to whatever cover there is. Many shooters totally neglect the importance of staying in the shade, yet this is one of the best forms of concealment there is. Animals, and people, really struggle to see what's in the shade when their eyes have adjusted to the light; try it yourself, the results are amazing.

Although less obvious, sound cover can be even more useful than visual cover, especially when you consider that the rabbit's sense of hearing is far superior to its eyesight. Listen to the ambient sounds and try to make the most of any that help to mask the subtle noises you generate as you move towards your target. The rustle of wind passing through the trees, the distant clatter of a tractor working the land, or the drone of passing aircraft are all sounds that rabbits most likely accept and can be used to hide your own. A farm I used to shoot on had a particularly productive rabbit warren on a steep bank that ran parallel to a busy dual carriageway. The heavy traffic created a rumble, which didn't exactly make for peaceful shooting, but it provided excellent sound cover that helped me bag bunnies despite some pretty clumsy stalking.

Reading your quarry's body language is another important part of the jigsaw and will tell you when to move and when to freeze. In fact, the stalker's mantra should be to 'move a little and look a lot'. If rabbits are feeding contentedly with their heads down, then it should be safe to proceed with caution, but stop as soon as one stirs. The first thing an uneasy rabbit will do is stop feeding; next it'll prick up its ears to test the air for sounds of approaching danger. When a rabbit becomes concerned enough to sit bolt upright, its companions will take notice and start to become unsettled. Give the rabbits further cause for concern and one will soon start to stamp its feet on the ground. This drumming signals danger and is usually the last straw, ending in the sight of fluffy white tails disappearing into the hedgerow as the alarmed rabbits dash for cover. The best advice is to keep still at the first sign of concern from the rabbits, and only proceed when they settle down again.

The final metres are always the slowest, and most nerve-racking. The tension and contortions of the stalk should have your heart pounding, and it's quite possible that you will have broken into a sweat, so it's worth taking a moment to calm down before taking the shot. More often than not, a successful stalk concludes with me crouching down for the extra stability of a kneeling shot. There is, however, a strong chance that you will be forced to belly-crawl during the demanding final stage of the stalk, especially if cover is thin on the ground.

Stalking on all fours is strenuous and uncomfortable, and there's every chance that you'll end up putting a knee, if not a hand, down on a cowpat or thistle from time to time, but there are benefits. Owing to the fact that you're sprawled on the ground, a belly-crawl improves your chances of going undetected and, when you make it to within range of your mark, you'll be able to make a super-steady shot from the prone position – as long as there's no tall vegetation in the way. Make sure the shot is a good one and you'll appreciate the true satisfaction of stalking. Although it's not the easiest way to target rabbits, it is by far the most rewarding – even if you do end up scratched and stinking of dung.

*You can keep your hands free by hocking rabbits and collecting them on the return journey.*

Once you've had a taste of success, you'll most likely want to trek on in the hope of adding another bunny or two to the evening's tally. Shot rabbits are a bit of a handful and trying to carry them will certainly compromise your ability to stalk with any degree of stealth. Using a game bag or backpack is preferable to having rabbits swinging from your arms, but I even find that too much of a burden when I want to weave my way unrestricted from one scrap of cover to another. Hocking is a useful solution that will allow you to hang shot rabbits in a safe place until you collect them on your return.

Hocking a rabbit effectively turns the legs into a handle and is very easy to do. Simply feel the part of a rabbit's hind leg behind the long foot, and you'll notice a bone and a tendon running parallel. Use your hunting knife to make a slit between the bone and tendon, and then hold the rabbit upside down with its hind legs either side of whatever you intend to hang it from – more often than not a branch or a discreet piece of wire fencing. Thread the foot of the uncut leg through the slit you made in the other until it pops all the way to the joint, which locks in place to create a secure fixing. It's wise to hock rabbits in an out-of-the-way place where they won't be spotted by walkers and can't be reached by marauding foxes.

# Time to switch to ambush tactics

Creeping to within range of a wily rabbit is about as exciting as air rifle hunting can get, and that's largely because it's so tricky. If you want an easier option, there is a far simpler way to put bunnies in the bag, and that is to sit and wait for them.

Ambushing, or static hunting, is a surprisingly easy way to outwit rabbits and it works a treat from late summer onwards when young rabbits are starting to wise-up. The hunter on the move has the odds stacked against him from the outset, simply because moving around is the number one best way to attract unwanted attention from your quarry. Even when wearing the best camouflage in the world, movement massively increases the likelihood of catching the eye of a wary critter. Admittedly, rabbits don't have the sharpest eyesight in the animal kingdom, but their vision is just a tiny part of their complex defence system. If they don't spot you, they still stand a very good chance of hearing you as you creep slowly through the fields, and their uncanny ability to detect vibrations through the ground means they can even pick up on what you believed to be a silent footfall. If all that doesn't make stalking difficult enough, there's the added problem of trying to ensure that the wind is in your face so your human scent isn't blown straight into your quarry's twitching nostrils. No wonder it feels like such a great achievement to bag a rabbit after a successful stalk.

For those of you who fancy taking the fast-track to rabbit stew, it pays to dispense with the idea of creeping within range of your quarry and play the waiting game instead. As a young shooter, I became thoroughly disheartened by countless failed stalks until the blindingly obvious solution dawned on me. After that *Eureka!* moment, I accounted for plenty of rabbits by simply sitting, or lying still until they ventured out within striking distance. The simple fact is that the static hunter is far less likely to be detected by the rabbit's aforementioned defences.

Nonetheless, a successful ambush depends on so much more than just sitting in a field in the vain hope that a suicidal rabbit will trundle out in front of you. Set up in the wrong place at the wrong time and you'd have been better off struggling with stalking, but with a little forethought, you should be able to engineer an ambush that results in several rabbits presenting themselves in front of you, and comfortably within range.

The most important thing is to ensure that you're targeting a spot that sees a reasonable amount of rabbity activity. Bunnies don't like too

*Rabbits don't have particularly good eyesight so only minimal cover is required for a dusk ambush.*

much disturbance around their burrows, and who can blame them? Stamp about above their network of tunnels and they may not emerge for a very long time, so it can pay to investigate initially without your gun. This way you can really capitalise when you sneak back a day or two later for a proper hunting trip.

During that reconnaissance visit, you'll want to gather as much information as possible to ensure that you set up your ambush in exactly the right place. Ideally, you'll time it so that you're there in the early evening when you should be able to see rabbits out frolicking in the weakening rays of the setting sun. Head back to the place where you saw most rabbits when you return with your gun and you should be off to a flying start.

Unfortunately, it's not usually that simple in real life: you may not be able to nip out for a recce at the prime time, or you may just happen to choose an evening when there aren't many rabbits

above ground. All is not lost, though, as there should still be plenty of clues to betray the presence of bunnies. Burrows are the next most obvious sign after an actual sighting. Look for the busy, well-worn ones with plenty of freshly excavated soil. It's safe to assume that rabbit holes that are blocked with dry leaves, twigs and other vegetation have been abandoned, so there's no point targeting these redundant burrows.

Droppings are a good sign of recent rabbit activity; the more dark and moist they are, the more fresh they are. Look also for the areas where the grass around the field margins has been cropped short by munching bunnies. If you find a well-grazed area like this, but fail to spot any obvious burrows, look for the patches of cover from which the offending rabbits are emerging. Closer investigation of patches of brambles, nettles, gorse or woodland will very likely reveal the runs that the rabbits use to travel between their burrows and their feeding grounds. These busy little highways can be prime areas to target and are well worth earmarking.

If you're controlling rabbits on a dairy holding, one place that I would recommend you don't target is a field that contains the resident herd of cattle. Apart from the obvious hazard posed by shooting close to livestock, the presence of cows can just be downright irritating. They can look inoffensive enough as they stand munching away on grass when you first arrive, but their curiosity quickly gets the better of them. Before long, you'll find yourself surrounded by a herd of inquisitive cattle, and once you've got their attention it's very difficult to shake them off. Shouting and handclapping may be enough to push the nosey old milkers far enough back to stop them slobbering over you or unintentionally trampling you, but it'll also be sufficient to terrify any rabbits within earshot. Unless cattle are being strip-grazed, in which case there should be an electric fence to keep them from getting too close to you, give them a wide berth.

When you have a promising, cattle-free, place in mind, you then need to work out where is the best place to hide in wait. If you aren't planning on shooting straight away, you can get away with causing a bit of disturbance. What I do is actually stand where I expect the rabbits to emerge and then look around for any areas of cover that might help to conceal a patient hunter. As I mentioned earlier, rabbits aren't gifted with the greatest eyesight, so it's unlikely that you'll need to construct a hide. Overgrown hedgerow margins often feature enough vegetation to hide a sitting shooter from sight, especially if you can position yourself in the shade. Sometimes the lie of the land is such that there just isn't sufficient cover along the hedgerow – this is when I tend to go prone. Rather than shooting along the hedgerow, I'll lay out in the field about 25 or 30 metres from where I expect the rabbits to show themselves. Shooting from the prone position makes for very steady shots, so it's likely that you'll be able to extend your hunting range – especially if you're using a pre-charged airgun mounted on a bipod. The downside is that lying on your belly can get uncomfortable, so I wouldn't recommend this position for long stints. You also need reasonably short grass so that your pellet can find its way to its mark without obstructions such as tall grass stems, nettles and thistles hampering its flight path.

I always make a point of tucking my trousers into my socks when I lie down to shoot – unless they're already tucked into my boots. The reason for this is because uncovered flesh is vulnerable to ticks when you're lying motionless in the grass.

*Dark, moist droppings are a sure sign of recent rabbit activity.*

*Freshly excavated soil confirms that a rabbit hole is in active use.*

Ticks dropped by deer can carry Lyme disease, so you really don't want to pick one up. Early symptoms, which can take weeks to develop, include a circular red rash around the bite. Unless treated promptly with antibiotics, later stages include temporary paralysis, memory loss, extreme tiredness, chronic joint pain, changes in personality and (not surprisingly when you've gone through that list) depression. Be warned!

Back to the hunt, I almost always wear a headnet and gloves when shooting from a lying position out in the field. Thus concealed, it takes very little natural cover to keep you from being spotted; a thick tussock of grass or patch of dock leaves should be enough to break up your profile and prevent you from rousing suspicion. From time to time, the grass is too long to take lying shots from out in the field when natural cover is scarce along the hedgerow. In this situation, I will occasionally go to the trouble of setting up a camouflage blind, suspended between two props. A screen of this nature is best positioned close to the hedge or at the base of a tree, so that its outline is softened by natural features of the landscape. Set the blind high enough that you can shoot from a sitting position, preferably with a beanbag seat stuffed under your backside, and you should be in for a comfortable evening's shooting.

Range estimation is another great advantage of an ambush. When hunting on the move, the shooter generally has to make an educated guess on the distance between himself and his quarry. The static shooter can be far more accurate, especially if you take the trouble to make a preliminary visit. When I'm planning an ambush, I'll pace out the distance from my hiding place to various markers around my target area. These markers could be trees, fence posts, nettle patches or any fixed object that I can use for reference. When a rabbit creeps out from the cover, I then use the closest marker to it to gauge the range and work out hold-over or hold-under accordingly.

The ability to work out range more accurately is also an advantage to less experienced shooters who are restricted to closer hunting ranges. In my early days, I couldn't shoot my old .22 Webley Vulcan very accurately beyond 20 metres, which is one of the reasons why I found it so hard to stalk within range. However, once I'd cottoned-on to the advantages of an ambush, I would simply locate a busy warren and then find a decent hiding place within 20 metres. When I returned to hunt one or two evenings later, I knew that any rabbit emerging from those burrows was within striking distance.

Shooting from a fixed position also allows you to ensure that your scent is being blown away from the rabbits. Human scent is notorious for putting rabbits to ground so I will happily compromise my visual cover and opt for a downwind hiding place to avoid early detection by bunnies' nostrils.

With a target area and hiding place in mind, it's just a question of leaving the spot undisturbed until you return. When the chance arises, I favour the last hour or two of daylight (the period of summer evening when swallows are replaced in the sky by fluttering bats) because rabbit activity usually picks up at the end of the day. With night approaching and the reduced likelihood of dog walkers being around, bunnies feel safe enough to venture out and feed on the dew-softened grass.

Head quietly to your chosen spot, keeping away from the target area in order to avoid causing undue disturbance to your quarry. If there are rabbits out, it's just as well to attempt a stalk as you close in: it'll help to keep your approach quiet, and if it ends in success there will be one less bunny to bolt down the burrow and alert the others to the potential danger. When you reach your hiding place, quietly settle into your spot and make yourself comfortable either in the sitting or lying position, then load-up and wait.

All being well, the wait shouldn't be too long; rabbits will be aware of the approaching night and should be keen to venture out to feed in the summer sunset. Sometimes you'll spot a rabbit creeping out from cover, but at other times they seem to appear from nowhere. You'll by watching

*A brace of bunnies taken during an early evening ambush.*

rabbit's eye and ear. The loud crack of a direct hit to the skull will often send any other rabbits running, but the lure of the sweet, green shoots of grass will soon draw them back.

Check through the scope that the rabbit is cleanly killed. If it is, leave it where it fell and sit tight. Stomping out over the warren will stifle your chances of further shots, so hold position and wait for more bunnies to emerge. It's surprising how confident rabbits can become as the evening advances, so there's every chance of making a good bag from your hiding place.

Typically, the hunter isn't always treated to the luxury of a leisurely reconnaissance visit prior to a shooting trip – work, family and countless other commitments frequently take care of that. But, even without methodical planning, static hunting is a very effective method for controlling rabbits, and all the same rules apply. There are often occasions when I'm out stalking rabbits and encounter a warren that is so busy that it would be foolish to move on. When you find a hotspot like this, great sport can be had by simply tucking yourself into the hedge or sprawling out in the field to wait for the rabbits to venture back out.

a spot intently, look away for a moment when your attention is distracted by a hunting kestrel or a bat clicking past, and then look back to see a rabbit sat nibbling, yards away from its burrow.

Owing to the careful preparation, taking the shot should be fairly straightforward – certainly a lot more straightforward than if you'd just stalked within range. You'll be in a stable position, your pulse won't be pounding and you'll have a very good idea of the distance to your target. Steady your aim to land the shot between the unsuspecting

As well as going undetected by rabbits, the static hunter is also less conspicuous to other wild animals, so keep a lookout for some interesting sights. Watch out for the barn owl silently ghosting along the line of the hedge in search of mice as the evening mist begins to gather, keep your eyes peeled for the amusing sight of playing badgers because these usually cautious mammals often venture out when they think all the humans have settled down in front of the television, and don't be surprised to see the occasional fox out hunting over the evening meadows. I've sometimes witnessed foxes making off with my rabbits just moments after I've taken a shot (testament indeed to the stealth and discretion of a silenced airgun) and I've watched one or two trot incredibly close while I've been huddled in the hedgerow. Just a couple of weeks ago, a large, glossy-coated dog fox wandered to within feet of me as I sat waiting for the rabbits to emerge. I could literally count the whiskers on old Charlie's nose when he finally caught my scent and froze. Seconds later, all I could see was the tip of his tail disappearing into the gloom as the wily scoundrel turned and scarpered after sensing that danger was close. Moments like this are among the hunter's greatest rewards.

# Long-range rabbiting

The improved accuracy resulting from the use of a bipod can increase effective hunting range considerably, especially when ambushing rabbits from a lying position. Although I don't use bipods with spring-powered airguns – because their recoiling action often becomes unpredictable when shot from a rest – there's no denying that the extra stability will significantly improve pellet grouping when using a pre-charged gun. In calm conditions, with no breeze to hamper accuracy, the legal limit airgun's effective range can be increased to well over 40 metres and, in the case of a high-powered FAC-rated airgun, that distance may stretch to beyond 60 metres.

But this sort of accuracy requires a lot of practise and perfect conditions to achieve, and I wouldn't encourage anyone to attempt such shots until they're absolutely familiar with the downrange performance of their rifle/scope/pellet combo. It has to be remembered that the air rifle hunter's quarry presents him with a comparatively tiny kill area that must be hit squarely in order to ensure a clean dispatch. For this reason, fieldcraft always wins over marksmanship, and I have a lot

more respect for the hunter who has the skill to get himself within 25 metres of his quarry than the man who takes a risky shot at long-range. That said, finely honed fieldcraft and expert marksmanship make for a deadly combination and a highly effective hunter.

When selecting a bipod, go for a good quality model – the ones made by Harris are excellent. Because I only tend to use a bipod when shooting from the prone position, I opt for the stability of a shorter six to nine-inch model with extendable legs. The adjustable legs are a tremendous help when setting up on uneven ground. It's also worth paying a little more for a bipod with a swivel feature that allows it to rock in its mounting rather than being fixed solid. This means that even if you don't have the legs set exactly level, you can still adjust the position of the gun to ensure that the vertical crosshair is perfectly upright when you're taking shots.

Most of the best bipods fit to the gun via a quick-release stud that's attached to the stock. Fitting these studs is fairly straightforward, but make sure you follow the manufacturer's instructions carefully, and always ensure that you remove the action of your gun from the stock before you drill the hole to accept the threaded end of the stud – cylinders of high-pressure air really don't mix well with drills. It's also worth going to the trouble of a test run: fit the stud to a piece of scrap wood so you can make sure you're using the right drill bits to exactly the right depth before you let rip on the woodwork of your cherished gun. Only on one occasion did I ever attempt to fit a quick-release stud without bothering to practise on a test block first, and the walnut stock still has the unsightly gouges to remind me that it wasn't a wise move.

Once you have your bipod fitted, you'll need to become competent with it. The boost this handy little gadget gives to your ability to shoot accurately should be immediately noticeable, but be patient before you start trying to stretch your hunting ranges. Contrary to some of the advice you may read, you don't have to embark on a strict fitness

*By getting low and using a bipod, the hunter can snipe rabbits at range from sparse cover.*

regime to achieve extra distance. Although being in reasonable physical condition helps with most aspects of hunting, I regard confidence and competence as the most important pieces in the jigsaw when it comes to marksmanship. In my opinion, the best way to achieve this is to get out and practise with the aim of achieving absolute familiarity with your combo. On the subject of familiarity, my ability to shoot accurately was at its pinnacle around ten years ago when I owned just one gun. Since then, the privileges of working as a shooting journalist have seduced me away from those days of airgun monogamy and I now own eight or nine different guns. Consequently, I'm not as familiar with my hardware as I was and I'm not as good at subconsciously predicting things like gun balance and trigger release points. It's something I'm trying to address.

Getting back on track, you need to practise on paper before you let loose on the rabbits with your bipod-mounted airgun. Set up targets at five-metre intervals out to 50 metres and you'll be able to work out the holdover required to keep pellets on target as they begin to drop away. A mil-dot scope, or any model with marked reference points along the reticules, will allow you to establish exactly where to aim at different distances, and remember that those points of reference will shift if you adjust the magnification. Once you've got your eye in and can hit the mark at longer distances in calm conditions, try shooting the same targets when there's a bit of a wind blowing – it'll provide a useful reminder of your limitations.

Many shooters are unsure of what to do with their leading arm when shooting off a bipod. The arm that usually supports the fore-end of the

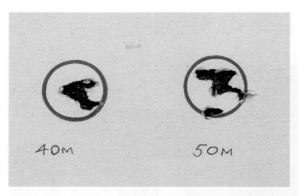

*The stability provided by a bipod improves grouping at longer ranges.*

*What would usually be the leading hand is dropped back to support and manoeuvre the butt of the gun when shooting off a bipod.*

stock (the left arm if you shoot right-handed) is suddenly rendered seemingly redundant as the weight of the gun is taken up by the bipod. Rather than habitually placing your spare hand around the fore-end or grabbing at the bipod, bring your arm back across your chest so that your fist sits beneath the butt of the shouldered rifle, which can be cradled between the thumb and forefinger. With the butt supported in this way, the gun is held with even more stability. The best thing about this technique is that by gently rolling and clenching the fist that's cradling the butt, you'll be able to raise and lower the gun to adjust your aim

by tiny increments. This fine degree of control will help to maximise the precision afforded by the support of the bipod.

When you're ready for the hunt, all the ambush tactics explained in the previous section still apply. The range-markers are even more important now, because there's a far greater margin for error between 30 and 40 metres than there is between 20 and 30 metres. In this situation, a laser range-finder can be really handy. Simply ping off the ranges to whatever set markers there are around the area you're targeting – cattle troughs, fence posts, trees and the like – and you won't need to go pacing over the burrows to work out the exact holdover required to land a pellet between your target's eye and ear over the varying distances.

For obvious reasons, you want a windless evening for long-range rabbiting, although a bipod will still improve your accuracy over shorter distances if there's a bit of a blow. Think about your own comfort when choosing a place to lie in wait for your quarry; being sprawled out on hard ground starts to become pretty unpleasant after an hour or so. Ideally, you want to get yourself on soft ground. Earth that has been baked dry by a hot summer can be hard as concrete, but it's bearable as long as it's relatively flat. Try to sprawl out on ground that has gone hard in the sun after being poached up by cattle and you'll soon find yourself experiencing some major discomfort.

What's really important is that the grass between you and where you expect the rabbits to appear is quite short. Hungry bunnies usually take care of this by grazing the grass of the field margins down to a short stubble, and it's a great help. Long tufts of grass and other obstructions pose a serious problem when shooting prone because you won't have the height to shoot over them, and even flimsy stems are enough to deflect a speeding pellet away from its mark. Short grass usually equals scant cover, but that's of little concern, as you should be sufficiently concealed when you're down on your belly. If you feel too exposed, put on a headnet to keep your face concealed.

When the first rabbit of the evening creeps out to nibble at the grass, don't be in too much of a rush to take the shot. You'll need to make calculations based on the distance to your target and the experience you gained on the practice range, so take your time. Slowly and calmly shift the gun until you're lined up, then study your target through the scope so you can make the necessary final adjustments before squeezing off the shot. Often, a rabbit that is unaware of your presence will settle to graze with its head down low – not a good profile when it comes to offering you a clear shot. Now is the time to remember the old trick of squeaking through your lips or clicking your tongue against the roof of your mouth. The noise should be enough to make the rabbit sit up on its hind legs as it twitches its ears to search out the source of the sound. A rabbit in this alert position, head-up, presents a very clear kill area.

As with any shot, you'll be subconsciously weighing up the risk as you study the sight picture

*Knowing the exact range to the target is more important than ever when distance is increased.*

– particularly over longer ranges. I won't pull the trigger unless I expect the pellet to strike where I want it to and, if the chance of missing seems recklessly high – because of wind, the distance or a fidgety target – I'll leave it. A miss is an irritating failure but wounding is something far worse. When doubt starts to creep in, you know it's a shot that's best left for another day.

# Rabbits after rain

The weather dictates the behaviour of quarry species more than most hunters realise. In extreme conditions, the effects are obvious: the survival instinct of wild animals forces them to seek shelter from heavy rain and to hole-up in shady places during times of searing sunshine. There are also more subtle instances that the hunter can capitalise on, one of these being the influence the weather has on the food supplies of pest species.

Rabbits will usually continue to feed through a drop of drizzle, but they rarely venture out during heavy downpours. After being confined to their burrows for several hours by prolonged rain, rabbits will be hungry and eager to feed, so expect them to venture out in numbers.

Summer rain after a dry spell is often followed by an even more enthusiastic binge. Apart from sending rabbits running for cover, significant summer rainfall usually prompts a new flush of growth that covers previously parched fields with lush green grass and clover. Rabbits are very partial to these tender young shoots and will often turn out en masse to feed on them, so it's well worth heading out after the showers have passed.

We had a very long period of drought in my neck of the woods last summer. The meadows were absolutely baked, and fields that should have been thick with green grass were reduced to a brittle thatch of parched yellow stems. There's no doubt that the effect the prolonged dry spell had on the grass impacted on the rabbit shooting. Bunnies were few and far between during daylight

*The rabbit shooter can expect action after summer rain has revived parched grassland.*

hours, and the only time worth targeting them was long after dark when a covering of dew had softened what remained of the grass, making it a little more palatable. Consequently, the bags I made during my daytime rabbiting forays were noticeably smaller than usual.

But the weather eventually broke and, as hoped, the desperately needed watering turned the meadows a rich, lustrous green. You could literally smell the sugar in the grass; the rabbits certainly could and they were soon out feeding in their droves where just a few days prior there appeared to be none. I made the most of the opportunity and filled the freezer after a couple of productive outings using both stalking and ambush tactics.

Another advantage of the softening effect that summer rain has on parched grass is that it tends to make it quieter underfoot. Tender green shoots yield fairly quietly to a careful footfall whereas they tend to flick against your soles and crunch beneath your feet when they're dry and brittle. Little things like this can make a huge difference.

# Retreat to the farmyard

High summer can be a seriously frustrating time for the air rifle hunter. The weather is warm and there is an abundance of vermin around, but successful shooting opportunities can be hard to come by during these long, hot days.

It's tricky because most of us are used to exploiting the peak hunting times around dawn and dusk. During these two 'magic hours', pest species behave fairly predictably as they venture out to fill their bellies either before or after catching up on a good night's sleep. Whether it's using a hide and decoys to ambush pigeons at dawn or trekking out across the fields to stalk rabbits at dusk, there are plenty of ruses to fill the game bag at these two ultra-productive periods at either end of the day.

And that's the problem with the dog days of summer: there is a lengthy, and often unbearably hot, period between dawn and dusk when hunting opportunities can sometimes seem impossible to come by.

At other times of year, the less productive chunk of the day between late morning and early evening is much shorter and can still provide frequent opportunities, but things are noticeably tougher now. Dry, hot weather will have baked the grass that pan-sized rabbits fed eagerly on throughout the day during spring and early summer, and they won't be venturing out until well after the cool evening dew has softened the parched pastures. The woodland can provide the air rifle hunter with shade, but you can bet your bottom dollar that the gnats and midges will be biting, and the frustration of trying to clock squirrels and pigeons hidden by the thick summer foliage before they spot you and scarper is enough to drive any shooter to distraction – even if the blood-sucking insects don't!

But there is a very comfortable, and often very productive, alternative that most people overlook, and that's the good old farmyard. A lot of people head for the shelter of farm buildings when it's raining, but I've fallen back on the farmyard countless times when the searing sun has made the open fields a thoroughly unpleasant place to be, and the outcome has always been surprisingly good.

Some landowners can be reluctant to let people shoot around their farm buildings, which is understandable when you consider that the farm provides a livelihood for them and their

*Farm buildings provide shade and sanctuary on days when hot weather makes hunting over open ground uncomfortable and unproductive.*

*A cool, shady cattle shed makes a comfortable base for pest control on a hot day.*

family. But most farmers also know that vermin can sometimes cause more harm around the confines of the farmyard than on all of their hundreds of acres of open land put together. Collared doves, feral pigeons, crows and jackdaws, plus the odd magpie and woodpigeon, will be nibbling their way through valuable grain stores plus any animal feed they can take advantage of. Not only are they eating into the farmer's profits, these avian pests also pose a hygiene risk by fouling water supplies and even food stores. Add an infestation of filthy rats to the equation, and it's difficult for any farmer not to consider the offer of some free pest control.

Let the farmer who owns your hunting ground know that you have insurance and are a responsible shooter and he is sure to take your approach seriously. Many landowners are at first reluctant to let people shoot around the farmyard because they are more familiar with rim-fire rifles and shotguns than airguns. So be prepared to give them a demonstration of what a quiet and accurate pest

control tool the air rifle can be in the right hands. The confines of the farmyard provide the sort of conditions in which the comparatively low power of air rifles really shines; so don't be afraid to make it known.

With permission secured, you can expect action to come thick and fast around farm buildings during the summer. Pest species don't enjoy uncomfortably hot weather any more than shooters do, and they'll also be retreating to the cool, dark buildings of the farmyard in search of refuge. When the weather is really hot, drinking troughs, and even puddles resulting from hosing down the yard or vehicles, will attract thirsty birds. Crows, magpies, feral pigeons and collared doves will often swoop in for a drink, as will woodpigeons when they're parched from feeding on dry, dusty corn stubbles. Tuck yourself out of sight in some shady corner overlooking one of these attractions and you could be treated to some red-hot action in the cool confines of the farm buildings.

# Woodpigeons in the cornfields

Some shooters would argue that going through all the motions necessary to decoy woodpigeons to within range of the air rifle defeats the simplicity that attracts many people to airguns in the first place. But, for those willing to put in the effort, I believe this form of shooting can really pay off – both in terms of satisfaction and in terms of the fine meat that can be harvested during a successful outing.

Rather than being a waste of time, I regard decoying woodpigeons as one of the most enjoyable summer hunting opportunities available to the airgun shooter. Admittedly, it doesn't always go exactly to plan, but it's a great feeling when it does. As with all air rifle hunting scenarios, the secret lies in getting close to your quarry. For this reason, time spent on reconnaissance is usually rewarded.

At this time of year, the pigeons on my patch are usually targeting cereal crops – most often wheat. At the start of the season, flat spots in cornfields caused by strong winds and heavy rain can be very productive areas. The flattening of the stems by harsh weather creates a landing and feeding zone where woodpigeons can easily access the nutritious grain kernels. When the birds really flock in, the damage is increased, and considerable acreages can be crushed so low that the crop (or what's left of it) is beyond the reach of the combine harvester.

The appeal of flat spots lies in the fact that they create a rich feeding opportunity in a concentrated area before the bulk of the crop can be reached. Set up a hide on the edge of a large flat spot and you could be in for a very rewarding day; just make sure you don't crush any more corn on your way there or you could jeopardise your shooting permission when the famer finds the trail of crushed corn left by your boots.

Later in the summer, decoying opportunities become far more abundant as an army of combine harvesters marches across the countryside, gathering the corn and reducing the tall stems to short stubbles. Amongst these stubbles lies a scattering of grain, either shed, crushed or missed by the combines. Pigeons instinctively recognise this food source and soon home in. Passing flocks can spot the flickering white wing feathers of feeding pigeons from literally miles away. This signal acts like a dinner gong, and hordes of them can quickly descend on a recently harvested field. For this reason, the remaining grain can be mopped up in no time, so the shooter has to act fast before the birds move on to pastures new.

Don't be in too much of a hurry, though. Before taking steps to set up a hide and decoys, it pays to spend some time watching the birds. A few minutes of reconnaissance should enable you to identify the flightlines the pigeons are using to move in and out of their feeding grounds. These flightlines are usually dictated by landscape forms such as the contours of hills and valleys, and even by prominent trees and hedgerows. The whereabouts of these 'pigeon highways' is critical because the birds can be very reluctant to deviate from them. Therefore, you want to get your decoy pattern right under an incoming flightline to ensure maximum action. Having identified these important entrance and exit routes, it's then time to turn your attention to exactly where you want to set up your hide and decoys.

*There's always corn left after the harvest, and pigeons will come flocking to feed on it.*

*Stealth and concealment are paramount when ambushing woodpigeons from a hide.*

Ideally, the decoy pattern will be set on a patch of ground that the birds have been hitting hard and the hide will be concealed in a hedgerow about 25 metres away – assuming that your shooting is sufficiently up to scratch to hunt at that range. The best way to stop a pigeon cleanly with an air rifle is to whack it in the head or directly between the shoulders, and the maximum range at which you are confident of achieving this will ultimately dictate the distance between your hide and decoys.

It isn't usually difficult to identify a stretch of hedgerow that lends itself well to hide building. What you're looking for is suitable natural cover into which you can weave your camouflage screen. I usually begin by clearing brambles and nettles from where I plan to sit, but only ever hack 'weed' species from the hedgerow and never cut hardwood species or anything that is making it stock-proof if you want to hang on to your shooting permission.

If the hedge is somewhat sparse, I'll throw a dark net behind my shooting position to act as a backdrop so incoming pigeons don't spot any chinks of light that may give the game away when I move. Next, the main front net is either hooked into the branches of hedgerow shrubs or draped from hide poles to create the main shell. It's a good idea to peg down the front of the net – either with tent pegs or pegs salvaged from deadwood in the hedge – this stops it from attracting attention by flapping in the breeze and the extra tension creates a bit more room inside. Then it's just a case of dressing the net hide with the weeds cleared from the ground to conceal its straight edges and help it blend in with the surrounding vegetation.

Other 'weeds' such as ivy, elder, burdock, cow parsley, nettles and the like also add to the effect, but don't go too mad with it because you will need clear 'windows' to shoot through.

Building a hide will create a significant amount of disturbance, but it can be done pretty quickly with a bit of practice. If you expect the birds to be targeting the same area for a few days, and are willing to take a gamble, it can pay to put the hide up in the evening and return for a dawn ambush. In my part of Somerset, woodpigeons and collared doves tend to feed hard after first light and then return to the woods later in the morning to digest their breakfast. This lull in activity can be exploited to throw up a hide before the birds return for their afternoon/evening binge if time is tight.

Unlike the shotgun shooter, air-gunners are limited to taking shots at static quarry, so pigeons have to be persuaded to actually settle among the decoys. It's a tall order but it's all part of the challenge. I've found that incoming birds quickly become spooked by moving decoys, such as 'flappers' and the like, but will settle among full-bodied artificials for long enough to allow me to compose a shot. It's a question of making the setup look as natural as possible, and I'm sure this is enhanced by having a variety of decoy styles rather than just a single shape of moulded bird. Look for variation between full-bodied decoys made by various manufacturers and try to obtain a few of each to make your flock look more animated.

My decoy flocks usually comprise at least ten, and as many as 15, plastic birds – I work on the 'more the merrier' principle. When setting out my decoys, I aim to create a fairly wide U-shaped pattern, as I have found that pigeons often land on the outside of a traditional V-shaped formation unless it is very wide. The plastic birds should be facing roughly into the wind, but don't line them up like soldiers. The natural appearance you want to achieve will be further enhanced by tilting some birds off at a slight angle to the wind, and mix up the gaps between them from as little as 18 inches to as much as eight feet.

Your decoys can also be set up to act as useful range markers. Working on the 25-metre premise, pace it out so the closest decoy is 15 or 20 metres from where you'll be hiding with the furthest 25 metres away. Now you know that any birds that land within the decoy pattern are within striking distance; the nearest and farthest decoys will also enable you to work out hold-under and hold-over for birds that present themselves at close-range and long-range.

With my pigeon decoys in place, I usually set up a plastic crow or magpie about ten metres further out in the field. Woodpigeons know that corvids are the wiliest of birds that won't settle where danger lurks, so the presence of a crow or magpie will give them added confidence. This additional decoy will also, from time to time, attract the occasional passing corvid, providing the opportunity to add one or two bonus birds to the bag.

With the trap set, it's time to settle into the hide and wait for events to unfold. If you have

*Pigeon decoys should be set facing roughly into the wind, but not lined up like soldiers.*

*Crow decoys can give pigeons extra confidence, and can also draw in the occasional bonus corvid.*

*Shots at decoyed woodpigeons are hard-earned – don't mess it up now!*

any doubt about the screen provided by your hide, pop on a headnet and gloves to improve your camouflage. Hopefully, birds should be dropping in fairly regularly, but the concealment of hide shooting means there's every chance of one or two very close, and often unusual, wildlife encounters to help pass the time.

When distracted by the thrill of the hunt, it's easy to forget little extras that can make the wait so much more comfortable. I'd say the most important of these is a bottle of water. Cornfields are hot, dusty places to spend time in the summer, even if you're sat in the shade. A pint or so of water will stop you from heading home early to quench your thirst or, worse still, throwing a wobbly because you've dehydrated yourself. A light snack will also be welcome, depending on how long you plan your shooting session to last, and a beanbag seat will quickly earn its keep. Sitting on bare earth is alright for a few minutes,

but you'll soon be fidgeting to alleviate the effects of a numb bum if you leave it much longer. The comfort of a beanbag seat will stop you from spooking birds as you jostle from buttock to buttock, and the added stability it provides will also improve your shooting – target shooters don't use these cushions for nothing.

When the birds do arrive, and when all goes to plan, the result can be breathtaking. The sight of 20 or 30 woodpigeons swooping into a pattern of decoys really sets the heart pounding. It's difficult to describe the excitement of watching the birds back-paddling with their wings open and feet stretched down as they descend among the deeks. When the birds have pitched, you can almost feel too scared to raise your rifle for fear of being detected by all those keen pairs of eyes. In all likelihood, though, the birds will arrive in smaller groups, but it is still pretty tense stuff, especially when one or two drop in really close.

It's now critical to stay calm and move slowly. Pick the bird that presents the easiest shot and poke the muzzle of your rifle through the hide until it's well clear of the netting and any vegetation. If your hide is well constructed, and your gun is a recoilless pre-charged model, you can use the netting as a cradle to make the shot really stable. A few words of warning, though: make sure you don't try to hang the gun from the barrel if it's of the floating variety. I've learned from experience that when supporting a floating barrel in this way, the weight of the gun can cause the net to push it up enough for shots to miss high. With many models of airgun, this is easily remedied by pushing the gun on through until the net is supporting the cylinder and not the barrel.

A head shot is usually my first choice for a clean dispatch when using a legal limit airgun. There's too much tissue and bone in the way to attempt a heart and lung shot from the front, although a strike through the shoulders, taken from behind, will find its way to the kill area. Pigeons' habit of constantly bobbing their heads complicates the shot to their skull, but they'll pause for long enough if you're patient. Even when feeding intently, pigeons frequently stop and look up to scan for danger – this is the time to nail that head shot. With the shot 'on', squeeze off very gently and watch carefully through the scope as you follow-through. Struck cleanly through the head, your selected bird should land flat on its face with the least of fuss and actually add to the appeal of the decoys. The muted report from your air rifle and the sound of the impacting pellet will probably spook the rest of the flock, but one or two birds – and sometimes the whole flock – will occasionally linger and offer the chance of a second shot.

Things don't always go perfectly to plan and there will be times when a bird falls belly-up or needs to be dispatched swiftly. At these times, it is essential to break cover, but this provides an ideal opportunity to retrieve any shot birds and add them to the decoy pattern. I use lengths of stiff plastic-coated gardening wire with the top inch stripped bare, or thin sticks sharpened at the ends, as props for shot birds. Spike the sharp end through the chin and stick the other end into the ground to hold the head up so they sit in a lifelike fashion.

Plastic decoys usually work but the real thing works much better; just remember not to set up the bird with its head held too high. An upstretched head, showing off too many of the white neck feathers, is the sign of an alarmed pigeon and will cause concern among others.

*Shot pigeons provide a lifelike addition to the decoy pattern.*

While you're out of the hide, clear any fine white feathers from the area around your decoys. Several of these soft, downy feathers are usually shed when a bird is shot. They stand out like a sore thumb on a bare stubble field, and pigeons know they're a signal of danger and will shun them. With the decoy pattern enhanced, and fear-inducing white feathers tidied away, you can slink back into the hide and hope for a few more incomers.

Of course, the pigeon decoyer isn't tied to using camouflage netting for a hide. There have been occasions when I've managed to clamber into the hedgerow where there's a hollowing wide enough for me to sit concealed by the shade and the leaves, and pick off pigeons without having to create any kind of screen that might make them suspicious. At other times, I've lain in a ditch, concealed only by the lie of the land and my camouflage clothing. Hiding in this way, with my head peering over the top, I once had a cracking time decoying pigeons and shooting them from the wonderful stability of a bipod, thanks to the fact that I was practically shooting from the prone position. The only problem was, despite the regular action, it was uncomfortable and I could only bear it for a couple of hours.

Sometimes the pigeon shooter is faced with the annoying situation of having an abundance of birds flighting around his patch, but none of them willing to land within range. It may be that they feel safer landing in an area way out in the field (far away from where foxes could be lurking in the hedgerow, and far away from anywhere you can build a discreet hide), or perhaps there's another flightline drawing birds away from the one you're trying to target. Whatever the reason, birds landing away from your area pose a problem that needs to be remedied or incomers will be tempted to join them rather than your decoys.

*Travelling light is not an option when decoying woodpigeons over cornfields.*

If pigeons are flying to a spot that presents a decent shooting opportunity, one very effective solution is to hunt with a friend and split up and target both areas. Two shooters hunting from two hides can really keep the birds moving back and forth, so there's potential to make a hefty shared bag as long as the shooting pressure doesn't force the pigeons to clear off altogether. If you're shooting on your own, the best option is to set up flags to scare the birds away from the corners of the field you're unable to cover, and hopefully divert them back to your decoy flock. My flags are nothing more sophisticated than carrier bags tied to three-foot lengths of garden cane so they flap in the breeze. I've also heard of shooters using pink or white balloons, working on the theory that they loosely resemble a human face, and I also know hunters who use the cheap plastic windmills sold in seaside gift shops for children to stick into sandcastles. You can use all sorts of things to create a flag or 'scarer' – the important thing is that it makes pigeons reluctant to settle nearby and diverts them back to you instead.

Make no mistake, though, there will be days when the whole laborious ritual of decoying pigeons fails miserably whatever you try. Nonetheless, if you get the groundwork right, you should succeed more often than not. And when it does go right, decoying pigeons to the air rifle is great sport. Yes, you'll have a heck of a lot of kit to pack up and lug back to the car, but you'll also take home with you the warm glow of success, and a few pigeons for the pot.

# Combine casualties

Pigeons aren't the only avian pests to be drawn to the cornfields around harvest time. Corvids, such as crows and magpies, are partial to snacking on grain, but they can also find more substantial pickings left in the wake of the combine.

The heavy machinery and sharp blades that batter the fields during harvest time inevitably cause their share of casualties. Mice, voles, shrews, rabbits and occasionally young deer fall victim to the onslaught as the habitat provided by tall corn stems is suddenly demolished. Scavenging corvids know this, and they soon home in to search out carrion left among the corn stubbles. Another feeding opportunity arises shortly after, when the balers have lifted and packed the remaining straw. This clearing of the ground exposes more remaining grain, as well as insects, slugs and worms, so crows and magpies will often return for another munch, as will the woodpigeons.

These opportunities are often short-lived – usually coming and going within a couple of days – and highlight the importance of keeping in touch with your shooting grounds. Most of us have busy lives and aren't in the privileged position of being able to spend as much time out on our patch as we'd like – that's certainly the case for me.

But you don't have to be there all the time to keep an eye on what's going on, and you don't necessarily have to be out with your shooting gear to gather information. I'm

*Expect to find gullible young magpies lurking close to where corn stubbles offer easy pickings.*

*A bunch of magpies bagged on the corn stubbles during a short summer session.*

fortunate in that one of my largest farm shoots runs alongside the road I drive along when travelling to and from work. Whenever I'm passing, I do my best to scan the fields and hedgerows for signs of quarry. And it's not unheard of for me to get home late for dinner after pulling over and taking a stroll to investigate whatever it was that caught my eye during the evening commute.

Just a few weeks ago as I write, a flurry of black and white in the corner of a sprawling field of wheat stubbles caught my eye as I was driving home. It was several weeks since the woodpigeons had swooped in to mop up grain left behind by the combine, and it appeared that they had now been replaced by a gathering of magpies.

I pulled over by a gateway and watched a family group of magpies foraging among the stubbles. This was clearly a hunting opportunity that would quickly pass, so I decided to return with the gun as soon as possible. By an amazing stroke of luck I passed a road kill rabbit on my way home. The festering bunny was way past its sell-by date, but to me it was prime corvid bait that would represent a combine casualty, so I stopped again and put it in the boot.

Back at home, I explained my predicament to my wife, who was surprisingly understanding and granted me a few hours shooting leave. A while later, I was back by the stubble field and relieved to see the magpies – half a dozen or so of them – were still flitting back and forth between the hedge and the stubbles.

There was no time to build a hide, and the disturbance would most likely have sent the birds fleeing, never to return. So instead, I decided to make the most of the cover provided by one of the big, round hay bales left in the field. I set out the rabbit (along with a magpie decoy to draw attention to the bait and convince the magpies that it was safe to return) within range of my hiding place and then sprawled myself out on the ground against my chosen bale. Once in position, I was frustrated to realise that I hadn't packed a bipod, which would have provided the perfect support for shooting

from the prone position. Nonetheless, I managed to fold my padded backpack in half to double its thickness and create a reasonable rest for the gun (necessity is, after all, the mother of invention and I have on several occasions used a folded-up jacket to similar effect).

To my surprise and delight, the spooked magpies returned sooner than I expected, and the backpack/rest provided sufficient stability for me to nail three greedy corvids before the rest of the clan realised it wasn't a safe place to feed and disappeared into the distance. It may only have been a modest bag, but it was a pleasing session and certainly brought home the importance of keeping in touch with farming practices on your shooting permission and responding quickly when opportunities arise.

# Thirst-quenching troughs

It is all too easy to fall into the trap of constantly relying on the same tactics for summer pigeon decoying. I often do it myself; constantly depending on a flock of deeks to draw pigeons within range when they're feeding over corn stubbles.

It's important to remember, though, that there are often times when a change from the norm (however subtle it may be) can have a massive influence on results. One example of this is targeting water troughs during the summer months. Pigeons in particular use up a lot of moisture digesting grain when they're feeding heavily over dry, dusty cornfields. This means that, from time to time, they're going to need a drink, and the easiest way to quench their thirst is usually by making a short flight to a nearby cattle trough.

I've already explained that water is one of the factors that draw pest species to the farmyard on warm days, and troughs set out in open fields are equally attractive. And it isn't just pigeons visiting cattle troughs for a sneaky gulp: crows, magpies and jackdaws will be seeking refreshment around

*A decoy will give confidence to incoming birds when thirsty pigeons swoop in to sip from cattle troughs.*

drinkers put out for cattle, pigs, sheep, horses and just about any other livestock. The appeal is even greater during spells of drought when natural water sources become particularly scarce.

Even if you don't actually spot woodpigeons or corvids drinking from cattle troughs, they leave plenty calling cards to betray their visits. Feathers on the surface are an obvious sign of the birds' presence, so look out for them. Another indication of avian visitors is their droppings on and around the trough. This is also another reminder of why

these birds are regarded as pests: the disease threat posed to livestock when water is heavily fouled is as much of a concern as the physical damage that pest species cause to crops.

Having identified what appears to be a busy drinking area, it's the usual case of setting up a hide or using natural cover to provide concealment within comfortable shooting range. When it comes to drawing birds in, there's nothing like the presence of a comrade to persuade them that the coast is clear and it's safe to return. So I usually set up a decoy (a pigeon deek if I'm targeting pigeons, or a crow or magpie if I'm after corvids) on the rim of the trough to pull them in.

Safe shooting is paramount, especially if there is any livestock in the vicinity of the trough. The implications of injuring a valuable farm animal or much-loved horse are almost unthinkable, but think about them you should, because it'll help you to ensure it doesn't happen. The safest option is to target drinkers in fields that don't have stock in them, or at milking time when the cows are in the yard or parlour if you shoot on a dairy farm. It is also most important to ensure that there's no chance of your shots damaging the trough. The rugged, old concrete drinkers are incredibly robust, and so are most of the heavy-duty galvanised ones, but it's still wise to make sure your shots don't strike them. You have to be incredibly careful around the cheap plastic troughs that are becoming increasingly popular on many farms. These vessels are brittle and flimsy, and offer no resistance to an airgun pellet. Damage a trough and the farmer will probably regard you as more of a pest than the birds you're supposed to be controlling, so make sure it doesn't happen. One way around this is to try and find a sitty tree that the birds are flighting to before fluttering down to the trough, and shoot them from there instead. Another is to put one or two decoys on the ground in the hope that inquisitive birds will present shots on the deck as they investigate the plastic deeks.

The use of flags can be as effective when shooting birds around troughs as when targeting them on the stubbles – and often more so. By and large, it's fair to assume that pigeons or corvids will be fairly evenly distributed between the various drinking points around your shoot. If there are half a dozen troughs spread across your ground, it stands to reason that you'll get more action around the one you're targeting if you set up scarers around the others. The flags I describe in the section on decoying pigeons in cornfields should help to ensure that plenty of birds turn up to drink at the trough that's closest to your hiding place.

# The mixed appeal of maize stubbles

Towards the tail end of summer, just as the days start to become perceptibly shorter and the evenings a little cooler, farmers will be getting themselves set for the maize harvest. British-grown maize doesn't really get enough sunshine to ripen sufficiently for human consumption as sweetcorn. Instead, the towering crop is usually harvested as a whole, pulverised by forage harvesters and then used to create maize silage, which is used as a feedstuff for livestock.

Just like the wheat harvest, the gathering of maize crops creates wastage that means a free meal for pigeons and corvids. As with other cereal crops, woodpigeons and collared doves will descend on the stubbles after the field has been exposed by the machines' blades, and maize also has a great appeal to crows, magpies and jackdaws. Seed-loving rooks are very partial to the large, nourishing kernels and will sometimes flock in great numbers.

Targeting birds over maize stubbles is usually done from a hide. The routine is the same as with other corn crops, so look out for those flightlines and position yourself accordingly. One of the biggest problems encountered when shooting over this terrain is that maize stems create a thick, fibrous (almost woody) shield that will easily deflect an airgun pellet way off its course. The best way around this is to study the lie of the land and try to find an elevated vantage point from which you'll be shooting over the tops of the stems rather than trying to thread pellets through them – it's a whole lot easier.

In terms of decoying, the choice depends on the pest species that you're presented with on the day. The previously explained corn stubble tactics will work for pigeons, and you can always set out one or two crow or magpie decoys a little further out from your plastic pigeon flock if you think a mixed bag is on the cards. If the fields are black with rooks, crow decoys should do the trick. As ever, shot birds are much better than plastic deeks once you've managed to bag one or two, so it's usually worth using a stiff wire or sharpened stick pushed through the chin to prop them up as naturally as possible. The bait and decoy technique described under 'Combine Casualties' should also work equally well if you encounter crows and/or magpies scavenging among maize stubbles.

Maize stubbles don't just attract birds, though. I've often witnessed grey squirrels clambering down from the trees and scampering out onto the open field to feed on the nourishing cobs left behind after the harvest. The cheeky little beggars had probably been raiding the crop for weeks but had been hidden by the dense, dark cover of the tall stems and thick green foliage. The absence of shielding maize plants turns the tables in the hunter's favour, and pest species often continue to venture out for some time, seemingly unaware of the fact that the sudden loss of cover has left them precariously exposed. Likewise, it's not unusual to encounter rabbits out feeding where maize stood a few days prior. These bunnies are sometimes surprisingly confident and, again, I can

only assume that they grow so accustomed to hiding among the thick jungle of stems that it takes them a while to realise that the harvest has exposed them. Stalking isn't usually an option because attempts to make a stealthy approach are likely to be hampered, either by the snap and crunch of the thick, brittle stems under your feet if the going is dry, or by the heavy clots of newly exposed soil that cling to your boots if there's been a drop of rain. However, a hide isn't always necessary in this situation: pull on your headnet and gloves and settle into the cover provided by the hedgerow along the field edge and you'll often be sufficiently hidden to snipe rabbits and squirrels as they venture out.

# Pigeons in summer woodland

I don't relish woodland shooting during the summer months. My main woodland shoot has a river running through it, and the combination of damp, muddy banks and a humid, shady

*Getting clear shots through the foliage is one of the biggest challenges of hunting in summer woodland.*

atmosphere creates the perfect breeding conditions for gnats and midges. I've tried wearing net suits and I've tried all kinds of insect repellents, but none of my efforts have prevented the tiny biting flies from trying to eat me alive when I venture into their realm during the summer. Therefore, I'm quite happy to keep myself entertained by shooting rabbits in the meadows and targeting pigeons and corvids on the cornfields until the first of the frosts have wiped out the swarms of flies in the woods.

The other reason I'm never particularly eager to venture into woodland during the warmest part of the year is the simple fact that it's so damned difficult to spot quarry. At this time of year, the trees are in full leaf and the dense foliage makes it virtually impossible to glimpse grey squirrels or avian quarry before they see me and clear off. The bottom line is that wily creatures stand a far better chance of eyeballing me as I stagger through the woods – cussing and swiping at the cloud of midges that has gathered around my head – than I do of spotting them as they hide behind a screen of dappled greenery.

There are a couple of exceptions, though. I have occasionally had great summer sport in woods that adjoin fields of cereal crops, though I try to stick to drier woods with fewer midges. When woodpigeons are hammering the corn, they'll often retire to the trees to digest the feast before heading back for more. Find a patch of woodland where bloated woodies gather for the late-morning siesta and you can expect to get a few shots

without having to go to the trouble of building a proper hide or setting out decoys. There's no need to venture out at sunrise, because the birds usually spend at least a couple of hours feeding before they head back to the woods. In terms of timekeeping, this sort of pigeon shooting is a civilised affair with the best of the sport usually coming between mid-morning and early afternoon.

What I do in this situation is target the trees on the outer edge of the woods, along the perimeter

*A caller can be used to draw pigeons closer as they flit beneath the canopy.*

*Woodpigeons don't usually make it this easy when the trees are in full leaf.*

of the cornfield. From inside the woods, you should be able to see the birds silhouetted against the sky as they swoop in from the fields. Try to find a place where the trees are more open and their foliage less dense, and it shouldn't be so tricky to spot pigeons and take clear shots once they've landed.

Of course, the cover provided by summer foliage isn't all bad and you should be able to utilise it to keep yourself out of sight. If there's been a long dry spell, the leaves and twigs on the woodland floor will be parched and brittle, so you'll not be able to move over them without making the sort of din that's bound to frighten your quarry. The trick is to set up in some shady place where you'll be able to pick off incoming birds without having to move about very much. Shade cast by the canopy of leaves means it's usually darker in the woods on a bright summer's day than during a grey day in the winter. For this reason, you're unlikely to need anything as elaborate as a net hide to keep you hidden. Put on a headnet and pair of lightweight gloves to hide your pink skin and you should disappear into your surroundings; covering up will also offer you some degree of protection against the midges if they get a whiff of your sweat and decide to go on the munch. If you do feel too exposed and in need of additional cover, you can make a very basic hide by leaning a few dead branches against the trunk of a tree - wigwam-

style. Although sparse, this arrangement is usually enough to break up your human outline sufficiently for you to go unnoticed.

The hunter can also target pigeons in the summer woods when the courtship ritual draws birds beneath the canopy. When overcome by the urge to mate during peak breeding season (from late spring through to the end of the summer), pigeons can often be spotted swooping from branch to branch among the lower limbs of the trees. Down on this level, they're far more vulnerable than when they're obscured by leaves in the uppermost branches.

Even if you don't see courting woodpigeons as they flit through the trees, their cooing usually betrays their approximate whereabouts. Sit patiently and a plump bird will eventually expose itself as it takes up a perch within range of your hiding place. For the impatient shooter, a pigeon caller can sometimes be put to good effect during this season. It can take a little practice to get right, and your early attempts could well spook more pigeons than they attract, but unseen woodies can often be persuaded to venture closer. Pose as a potential mate by using a caller to mimic their cooing, and amorous woodpigeons can be seduced to within range of your rifle.

# Sit and wait for squirrels

Summer squirrel control can be taxing to say the least and it often feels like the odds are stacked against you from the outset when thick leaf cover makes it almost impossible to spot quarry.

Hunting on the move is far less productive than it was in the spring for the simple fact that summer conditions usually enable squirrels to see and hear you crunching across the parched woodland floor long before you manage to catch a glimpse of them sat amongst a shroud of green foliage. More often than not, the crafty little bushy-tails will be completely hidden from eyeshot by the time you pass by, and this often

*A net screen provides a backdrop while ambushing squirrels along the edge of a pheasant release pen.*

gives the impression that the woods are a barren place, devoid of quarry and really not worth committing time to during the warmer months.

But pause in the right place for a while and you could be presented with a very different scene. Although the woodland falls silent at the lumbering arrival of the hunter, wild creatures soon venture back out when the danger appears to have passed. Wait and watch and the squirrels will start going about their business again: first just peeping out from their hiding places to check that the coast is clear, and before long clambering through the branches and scurrying amongst the leaf litter. This time the advantage is yours; your quarry's movement will reveal its whereabouts while you sit motionless, undetectable and ready to strike.

The success of any ambush in summer woodland (any ambush at all for that matter) depends very much on being in the right place. The main criterion is a decent field of vision: dense shrubbery will hem you in, restricting your field of view and hampering your ability to spot quarry and deliver clear shots, so look for open areas from where you can cover the open boughs of mature trees.

Glades and rides are excellent areas to target in the summer. Such places are deliberately kept clear by foresters or shoot managers to either provide access tracks for vehicles or to improve wildlife habitat by letting in light and adding diversity to the woodland environment. Set up in a place like this and you should be able to observe, and get unobstructed shots into, the flanking treetops. Natural glades where the canopy has been opened up by wind-blown trees provide similar opportunities, as do the outer boundaries of pheasant release pens. Low cover is kept in check by relentless scratching by foraging pheasants on the inside of these pens, and it's often deliberately cleared from the perimeters to stop predatory mammals from climbing in, and to reduce the chance of falling branches breaching the boundary fence.

Apart from resulting in relatively open patches of woodland, the fence line also creates a highway for quarry. Wild creatures tend to follow edges (just think about the way rats hug the walls around farm buildings) and you'll often encounter squirrels following the course of the wire netting around the release pen. It's this inclination to follow the line that prompts the gamekeeper to set his traps tight to the outer edge of the fence, and you can also exploit it to catch your quarry on the hop.

Set up within shooting range of a blind corner on the release pen fence and you can expect to get shots at squirrels as they creep round. Rats and rabbits are also likely to follow the same route, and remember to pay attention to what's going on above the ground, too. You'll sometimes see squirrels sitting on top of a fence post or clambering through the interlinking branches to move between the trees inside and outside the pen.

Setting up this sort of ambush in summer woodland is usually quite straightforward because there's plenty of natural cover. Squirrels are nothing like as sharp-eyed as most avian quarry species; they certainly aren't as spooked by the sight of a face peering out from the undergrowth, and tend to rely on movement and sound to clock predators. However, I sometimes set up a basic net hide to create a screen behind me if I have to position myself away from sufficient cover in order to find a place that offers me clear shots. This hide is a very basic affair, though, and I don't go to the trouble of dressing it with foliage. What I do is set up a couple of hide poles (or wooden poles cut from hazel sticks) behind me and drape the net from them to create a backdrop, which reduces the chances of my silhouette catching my quarry's eye when I move to raise the gun. If I can get away with it, I keep the distance between the poles quite short so I can double up the net for extra thickness, and also ensure that it has the proper 'outside' leafy pattern on both sides.

Preparations are minimal and, once the backdrop is set in place, it's simply a matter of making myself comfortable and waiting for the woodland to settle down from the disturbance of my arrival. The return of the birdsong is usually the first indication that the residents are venturing back out, and I wouldn't be surprised if squirrels use this chorus as their cue to return to whatever they were doing before I came tramping along. This is the time to listen very carefully, especially if it's a calm day, because the gentle click of claws on dry bark, the swish of a swinging branch, or a rustling amongst the dry leaves will often signal the whereabouts of a squirrel. The tables are turned now, for you're the one who is sitting silently with little chance of being detected.

The success of these sessions depends very much on your ability to sit patiently, and to tolerate the irritation of the summer midges if you choose to venture out on an evening when these nasty little pests are biting. Whatever the conditions, the chances are that you'll get more opportunities by sitting it out than by roving through the woods. And if you do bag a few squirrels, remember to keep their tails. These furry trophies are gratefully received by trout fishermen who use the fibres to tie their own imitation fly hooks, and can also be shown to your host as evidence of your commitment to summer pest control.

# Recipes for summer

### WARM PIGEON SALAD WITH PINE NUTS

Pan-frying is often thought of as the classic method for cooking pigeon breasts, and the result is regarded in culinary circles as something of a delicacy. It may not come cheap in top-notch restaurants, but pigeon shooters can enjoy this sumptuous dish for free.

This is a very simple recipe that is great for a starter or as a summertime snack that's ready to serve in about 10 minutes. The fresh green salad leaves work well with the strong, dark meat and the pine nuts give it a lovely crunch.

*To serve 2*

**Ingredients**

Breast meat from 2 woodpigeons
Olive oil
55g pine nuts
Mixed salad leaves – include rocket for a peppery bite

**For the vinaigrette**

2 tablespoons of olive oil
2 tablespoons of white wine vinegar
1 heaped teaspoon of Dijon mustard
1 tablespoon of runny honey
Salt and pepper

Begin by making the vinaigrette so you can pour it over the salad as soon as it's served. Simply put all the ingredients in a jar with a twist of salt and pepper and give it a good shake to blend.

Heat a small dash of olive oil in the frying pan and toast the pine nuts, taking care not to let them catch and burn. Once browned, set aside on a sheet of kitchen roll.

Season the pigeon breasts with salt and pepper, and fry with another dash of olive oil. Turn after 3 minutes and cook for a further 2 or 3 minutes, depending on how rare you like them.

Remove the pigeon breasts from the heat, slice thinly and arrange on a bed of salad. Scatter pine nuts over the top and then drizzle the vinaigrette over. Serve with crusty bread and butter.

## BUNNY BARBECUE

Rabbit shooting yields fine meat for the table, and often lots of it when the weather is fine. Typical dishes like rabbit stew and casseroles are great winter warmers, but bunny meat can also form the basis of a delicious summer barbecue.

When it comes to kebabs, you can use chunks of rabbit just as you'd use chicken. Once loaded with onion and peppers and chargrilled, your friends won't even notice the difference. And, if you're feeling more ambitious, rabbit meat can also be used to make your own delicious burgers.

After paunching, skinning and jointing rabbits, I leave the meat to soak overnight in the fridge. All I do is place it in a large bowl, then cover with cold water and add a couple good pinches of salt and a slosh of white wine vinegar to create, what is best described as, a brine. This solution draws impurities out of the meat and reduces the bitterness that can sometimes taint the flavour of rabbit.

After draining off the water, I then use a small, sharp knife to trim the best pieces of meat from the bones. The chunkiest cuts are kept for kebabs and the smaller scraps go into the mincer to make the basis of my bunny burgers.

The two recipes below use three rabbits to feed four people very generously.

## BUNNY BURGERS

### Ingredients

Meat from 1 large rabbit (jointed and boned)
170g pork belly
3 tablespoons of marmalade
Breadcrumbs (the ready-made ones are fine)
A handful of flour
Herbs (dried or fresh from the garden)
Salt and pepper

Trim and discard the skin from the pork belly, then dice and run through a mincer along with the rabbit meat. Transfer into a large bowl, add the marmalade and chopped herbs, and then season with salt and pepper.

Roll up your sleeves and mix the ingredients thoroughly with your hands. Add the breadcrumbs a few at a time until the mixture stiffens to a workable consistency. Use your hands to separate the mixture into apple-sized balls, roll in flour and then pat to form burgers between 2cm and 3cm thick.

### To cook

Grill for 5 or 6 minutes on each side, or until cooked right through. The sugar from the marmalade will caramelise to create a dark, crispy crust.

Serve in baps with salad and coleslaw or whatever sauce you fancy.

## RABBIT KEBABS

### Ingredients

Best meat from 2 rabbits (jointed and boned)
1 red onion, roughly chopped
1 red pepper, roughly chopped
170g mushrooms, roughly chopped

### For the marinade

2 tablespoons of olive oil
2 tablespoons of white wine vinegar
2 tablespoons of honey
1 clove of garlic, crushed
Half a lime
A fistful of fresh herbs
Salt and pepper

Start by making the marinade. Tip the oil, vinegar, honey and crushed garlic into a jar, then add a good squeeze of lime, the roughly chopped herbs and season with a generous grind of salt and pepper. Screw on the lid and give it a thorough shake to mix all the ingredients.

Place the chunks of rabbit into a bowl, then pour the marinade over the top and mix with your hands to ensure an even covering. Cover the top with cling film and place in the fridge for an hour or so – or overnight to really infuse the flavours if you have time.

Thread the marinated meat onto kebabs with the roughly chopped onion, pepper and mushrooms.

### To cook

Place on a hot grill and turn regularly. They should be cooked right through in about 12 minutes.

## PIGEON BOLOGNESE

Mamma Mia! This woodpigeon dish has an Italian twist that gives it a very summery feel – though it's great throughout the year.

The fact that the pigeon is 'disguised' in a robust sauce also means children will gobble it with gusto. Serve it with garlic bread and a generous topping of Parmesan cheese, and even the most stubborn members of the 'I don't like game' brigade will be coming back for seconds. I also appreciate this dish as a refreshing break from the norm when the pigeon fatigue starts to set in after a long run of good days over the corn stubbles, and an equally long stint of pigeon-based meals.

*To serve 4*

### Ingredients
Breast meat from 3 woodpigeons
225g minced pork
Olive oil
2 onions, finely chopped
2 cloves of garlic, crushed
1 stick of celery, finely chopped
2 medium carrots, finely chopped
2 red peppers, finely chopped
2 tins of chopped tomatoes
1 large glass of red wine
2 beef stock cubes
1 tablespoon of dried mixed herbs
Salt and pepper

Pass the pigeon breasts through a mincer – you can use a food processor if you don't have a mincer, but be careful not to blitz the meat into a paste.

Splash some olive oil into a large pan or wok, and gently fry the finely chopped onions, celery, carrots and peppers, until they begin to soften. Crush in the garlic and add the minced pigeon and pork, then fry until brown. Pour in the tinned tomatoes, red wine and herbs, and cook until simmering gently. Crumble and stir in the stock cubes and continue to simmer gently for 1 hour, stirring occasionally and adding more wine or water if it begins to look dry.

Season to taste and serve on spaghetti with Parmesan cheese and a good twist of pepper.

# AUTUMN

*Nothing stirs the hunter-gatherer instinct like the arrival of autumn: the beautiful golden colours, that noticeable nip in the air, and the gradual drawing in of the evenings. These signals trigger an indescribable urge to be out in the countryside, crunching through coppery woods and plundering the autumn harvest. It must hark back to our ancestors' very real need to make the most of every last morsel of available nourishment in readiness for the lean and testing months that lie ahead.*

*The seasonal shift also seems to have the same effect on quarry species; the abundance of fruit and nuts sending them into a foraging frenzy and creating a wide variety of opportunities for the hunter.*

# Rabbits and mushrooms

The short period of the year that foragers regard as prime mushrooming season is also a wonderful time for stalking rabbits. It's that period of limbo before autumn really kicks in: when the days are getting noticeably shorter, but there's still just enough daylight to get out with the gun after work.

Mushroom pickers will recognise this time as the few brief weeks before the first frosts arrive and turn their harvest to mush. For shooters, it's a time when young rabbits from the summer litters have made some decent size, but are still rather uneducated on the realities of life, and death, and not too wary. These 'harvest' bunnies are perfect for the pot; three-quarters grown and wonderfully tender.

My early autumn rabbit shooting sessions tend to make more of a contribution to the kitchen than the pest control campaigns. With an hour, or two at the most, to spare for a mid-week stroll around the meadows, I'm usually pleased to go home with one or two rabbits for the pot – and a few mushrooms too, if I get lucky.

In all honesty, these snatched evenings in pursuit of rabbits are more about being out there than making big bags. This is a magical time of year, when it suddenly becomes very apparent that warm evenings in the field will soon be lost to the long, dark nights of winter – so make the most of them.

More often than not I'll be on the move, stalking rabbits using the tactics I described for the summer months. One of the biggest obstacles to overcome is the heavy dew that falls at the end of these ever-shortening days. The moisture on the grass makes for slippery going and you have to keep your wits about you if you're going to stay on your feet, especially when negotiating steep ground – and why is it that the descent is always more treacherous than the ascent? The moisture caused by dewfall also tends to make the rubber soles of your boots squeak against the damp blades of grass, adding an extra degree of difficulty to the stalk. It's not such a problem when there's a gentle wind creating a little background noise, but it can be a real nuisance on calm, silent evenings.

From time to time, I'll decide to settle down and wait in a place where I've spotted a few rabbits. Like us, the bunnies realise that the days are getting shorter and they too want to make the most of what remains of the settled weather. If your arrival sends frightened rabbits running to ground, it's a fair bet that they'll soon be venturing back out to enjoy the last precious rays of sunshine before dusk closes in.

There seems to be an absolute abundance of wild creatures about on these early autumn evenings, and some of my closest encounters with wildlife including deer, barn owls, hares and badgers have

*A rabbit and mushrooms provide the basis of a tasty meal – as long as you know what you're picking.*

occurred while out on these evening rabbit rounds (especially if I decide to sit down amongst the cover and wait). You should also be prepared for unexpected encounters with quarry.

Magpies in particular tend to venture out in numbers as the light turns from the soft golden glow of early evening to the cold blue haze of dusk. These cool, dewy evenings tend to be synonymous with abundant hatches of crane flies (also known as daddy-long-legs) from the long, damp meadow grass. These gangly insects are regarded by magpies as something of a delicacy and can attract fairly large groups of these opportunistic corvids. There's been many a time that I've bagged one or two bonus magpies while lying in the damp grass waiting for the rabbits to creep back out.

Another potential bonus is the chance of finding delicious field mushrooms popping their heads up through the grass. This is an opportunity too good to miss as these wild 'shrooms are delicious either simply fried in butter or added to a recipe with the rabbit you'll hopefully be taking home with you. I try to keep a carrier bag stuffed in my pocket for gently transporting mushrooms back home, because they'll get smashed into a gooey mess if you try to stuff them into your pockets. However, there have been occasions when I've been caught on the hop with nothing to carry the evening's pickings in: your camouflage headnet will serve as a suitable makeshift mushroom sack on such occasions, and is equally good for blackberries if you don't mind it getting stained.

Anyone considering combining a hunting trip with a fungus foray is advised to note that edible horse mushrooms and the poisonous yellow stainer look almost identical. My advice is to buy yourself a comprehensive illustrated field guide and don't eat anything you pick unless you are absolutely certain that it's safe to do so. Better still, find someone with mushroom-picking experience and ask him or her to show you.

Eat yellow stainers and your body will want to rapidly flush this poisonous fungus from your system. Expect a violent evacuation of the offending mushrooms, and anything else you try to eat or drink, over the next few hours. I've heard reports of cases of poisoning where sickness and diarrhoea have been so severe as to cause serious dehydration and even hospitalisation.

There's a method for telling yellow stainers from horse mushrooms, but the differences are very subtle unless you have both to hand. Yellow stainers turn bright yellow when bruised but, after a moment, the staining fades to brown. Horse mushrooms stain yellow, but not as brightly, and the yellow persists and does not turn brown. Also, the base of the horse mushroom's stem does not turn yellow when bruised, on the yellow stainer it does. If in any doubt, leave them well alone and stick to a supper of rabbit and shop-bought mushrooms, which won't turn your stomach inside out.

# The pheasant release pen

Once the leaves begin to turn and fall, I gradually shift my attention back to the woodland. Week after week, the foliage is thinning and it's getting easier to spot quarry in the trees.

My autumn woodland campaign tends to start around the pheasant release pen. Most of my shooting permissions are shared with pheasant shooters and, in the grand scheme of things, I am regarded as their pest controller. Many of the pest species are drawn to the release pen so it's usually a productive place to linger.

Gamekeepers on grand estates and members of smaller shooting syndicates pride themselves on their pheasant release pens. These sprawling enclosures are like fortresses, protected by six-foot chicken netting, electric fencing and a battery of traps to prevent foxes, stoats and weasels from bumping off their precious pheasants. During the summer, young pheasant poults are released into the relative safety of these pens, usually in their hundreds and often in their thousands, to

*Step inside a pheasant release pen and you can expect to encounter a variety of pest species.*

acclimatise to the woodland environment before the shooting season gets underway later in the autumn. The pen acts as a safe haven while the chicken-brained pheasants gradually learn the realities of life in the semi-wild before being allowed to rove further as they grow and mature. Confinement to the pens also helps to make pheasants territorial and reduces the risk of them straying onto someone else's ground when they're eventually granted more freedom.

Unfortunately, most landowners are no longer able to afford to employ a team of gamekeepers to keep pests at bay. A single full-time keeper is now regarded as something of a luxury, and on many smaller shoots volunteers do the work. Consequently, pests like rats, grey squirrels, crows and magpies can have rather an easy time around the release pens, helping themselves to the grain put out for the pheasants.

*Pheasant release pens act like magnets to vermin – and the gamekeeper's traps are testament to that.*

It's not all bad news, though, as the need for an alternative pest control solution opens a door for the air rifle hunter. Speak to a busy gamekeeper or the manager of a cash-strapped shooting syndicate and there's every chance that they'll welcome the offer of some help with reducing the numbers of unwanted guests.

Shooting around release pens is fairly straightforward because pest species will be drawn towards the places where feed is put out. All you need to do is set yourself up in a spot that enables you to target these feeding stations while posing no threat, and causing minimal disturbance to the pheasants. It may be more suitable to target the trees that birds are flighting to before they swoop down to the feeders, or try to find the overlapping branches that squirrels use to clamber from tree to tree and over the perimeter fence on their way to the banquet. Squirrels will also scramble straight up and over wire netting, especially if

there's a point where a fallen branch has become propped against the fence to create a helpful ladder for them. If you find a place like this, it could well be an established route that will produce several shots during your visit. Just remember to take the branch down and straighten out the fence before you leave to make it a little bit harder for pests to clamber back in when you've gone.

If possible, I prefer to use natural cover to keep me hidden because it's so much more discreet than building a hide. However, there are times when it can be worth setting up a screen or arranging a few dead branches to keep you hidden within range of a particularly productive area. Quarry species can be quite confident around these hot spots, and it's a situation in which a pop-up hide can be used to provide a quick fix for the hunter in need of concealment. Although these hides aren't the best when it comes to blending in with the natural world, they do provide the added luxury of a waterproof shell if wet weather is forecast.

# Fruitful hunting

The arrival of autumn is usually a bountiful time for the air rifle hunter. Quarry species are abundant at this time of year, and you can expect to encounter a few gullible young'uns from the summer broods. Furthermore, all wild creatures are busy making the most of a glut of natural food, building up their reserves in order to maximise their chances of surviving the harsh winter weather that lies ahead.

Locating these autumn food sources can bring great rewards to the hunter. Places where food is plentiful can attract a tremendous concentration of quarry: species like grey squirrel, woodpigeon and even wily corvids are often far less wary than usual when their attention is diverted by the sudden abundance of easily obtainable food.

*Beechmast will attract woodpigeons, jays and squirrels as the woodland floor provides a banquet amongst the leaf litter.*

Many trees and shrubs around your woodland shoot will be heavy with fruit, and even after they've shed this year's harvest, birds and mammals will still be foraging among the leaf litter for any hidden leftovers. Lots of the fruit and nut trees worth targeting are common

knowledge, but some of the less obvious ones can be equally attractive to hungry creatures.

Acorns, beechmast and hazelnuts usually feature at the top of my list when I'm planning a sortie around an autumn food source. Hazelnuts are a firm favourite with grey squirrels and time spent lingering around the hazel coppice will often be rewarded when squirrels are gathering nuts for their winter cache.

As an interesting aside, holes nibbled in hazelnuts can reveal the presence of one of Britain's rarest mammals: the dormouse, a tiny rodent, which is listed as an endangered species. Their favoured habitat is mature deciduous woodland, and they could be present on your woodland shoot.

Although dormice are nocturnal and hardly ever venture down onto the ground, it's quite easy to find their telltale signs dropped on the woodland floor if they're present. These little mice leave very distinctive bite marks on hazelnut shells while they're nibbling through to access the kernel inside. Dormice make a small round hole with a very neat inner rim and leave tooth marks running at an angle to the surface of the shell. If you find tooth marks on the inner rim of the hole but none towards the nut's surface, it's probably the work of a bank vole. Tooth marks on the inner rim and rough marks on the surface of the nut are the munchings of a wood mouse, and you can be fairly sure that nuts, which have been smashed open (usually in half and with jagged edges) are a grey squirrel's leftovers.

As appetising as hazelnuts are to all sorts of wildlife, acorns and beechmast also have great appeal to grey squirrels and avian quarry. Find a stand of oaks or beeches where the ground is littered with these nourishing morsels, and it's very likely that you'll find woodpigeons rummaging alongside greedy squirrels. Keep yourself well hidden and there's a good chance of encountering jays too.

Acorns are fairly easy to spot on the deck but, to the casual observer, the rustling carpet of the beech wood looks like nothing more than a pile of decaying leaves ... look closer and you'll see much more. Beeches will have cast their nuts (known as beechmast) onto the ground in early autumn, creating an important food reserve for wild creatures. Beneath the four lobes of the hard bristly shell of the beech nut lie the pointed kernels. These tasty little morsels are so nutritious that in the past farmers would turn their pigs out into the woods where they could forage the free crop. The practice is uncommon now, but birds and animals including nuthatches, bramblings, badgers and wood mice are quick to home in on the beechmast harvest. Several of the air rifle hunter's quarry species also know that the protein-packed kernels will help to sustain them through the colder months; always be on the lookout for grey squirrels, woodpigeons and jays around beeches.

Subsequent leaf-falls will eventually bury much of the beechmast, but remnants of the main crop will linger into the new year. Although it's always important to scan the trees for activity, don't neglect the ground; squirrels in particular can often be encountered as they rummage through the leaf litter in search of any remaining kernels.

Although often overlooked by hunters, walnuts and sweet chestnuts also feature high on the nutty menu. If you're lucky enough to have a mature walnut tree or two on your shoot, you should expect to encounter more than a few grey squirrels in its vicinity as summer turns into autumn. Sweet chestnuts are usually left until a little later in the year. When the leaves begin to take on their golden autumn hue, the fruits of the sweet chestnut are usually too green and spikey for squirrels to tackle, but hungry tree-rats will return to feed on the tender nutty centre after they've turned brown and fallen to the ground. Fallen sweet chestnuts are often ripe enough to

*This dragonfly became ensnared in a cobweb among the ripening hedgerow fruit. Magpies seek out morsels like this in the autumn.*

split open by themselves, and you'll also find pigeons and jays investigating the woodland floor when these nutritious nuts are scattered among the leaves.

Even crops of blackberries, elderberries and sloes can draw in quarry species. I've occasionally seen woodpigeons feeding on these dark, fruity berries, but I more often regard them as a magpie attractor. I'm not sure how keen magpies are on the actual fruit, but they know that this juicy, sticky hedgerow crop attracts all sorts of tasty insects for them to munch on. Get up at the crack of dawn and take a look at the cobweb-covered hedgerows, and in those cobwebs you'll find all sorts of creepy-crawlies. Among the bugs, you can expect to see trapped crane flies, moths and even dragonflies, attracted by the sweet juices of the fruit and ensnared by the clinging web. Magpies know this and often patrol the fruit-bearing hedgerows at first light in search of trapped insects for breakfast. Be there with a hide, and perhaps one or two magpie decoys, and you're likely to be rewarded.

And if you see a heavy crop of red hawthorn berries when you're nosing around the hedgerows, bear the spot in mind for later in the year. Hawthorn berries are tougher than most hedgerow fruit, and for this reason they don't

*Even the wily jay can be outwitted when distracted by an abundance of natural food.*

seem to be as popular with birds and mammals, but it also means they stand up better to frost. Once winter has tightened its grip and food reserves begin to run low, you'll often find woodpigeons resorting to hawthorn berries for nourishment, especially if a covering of snow or frost prevents them from finding food on the ground. Another bonus is that pigeons taste great when they've been feasting on hawthorn. Bag a couple of birds that have their crops stuffed with these bright crimson berries and you know you're in for a tasty meal.

How you target these food sources will vary from situation to situation. Sometimes the attraction is so great, and the visits by quarry species so frequent, that it's worth setting up a hide. At other times it's possible to find sufficient natural cover to help keep you concealed. More often than not, I opt for natural cover because these food sources can disappear as quickly as they arrive, so there's simply not enough time to construct a hide.

However you go about targeting pest species around ripening fruit and nuts, the appeal of these seasonal banquets is undeniable. Keep your eyes peeled for nuts and berries as autumn unfolds so you can make the most of the opportunities provided by nature's wild harvest.

# Exploiting the autumn frenzy

There's no doubt about it, the rich pickings of autumn bring with them plenty of opportunities for the hunter. Woodland creatures are busy making the most of the exceptional abundance of food, laying down reserves for when times get decidedly tougher. The easy pickings attract all sorts of pest species, so expect the day's bag to be varied with a good chance of featuring something for the pot.

When I head to the woods in the autumn, I like to travel light. Bulky equipment like decoys and hide-building kit usually stay at home; all I take is what I can easily carry. After my airgun and a pocketful of pellets, the most important gear is my clothing because I'll be relying on it for concealment. My usual choice is a tree-print camouflage jacket and a pair of green or camo trousers, and I certainly don't worry about making sure that all my camouflaged garments have matching patterns. In fact, I think it's better if they don't because then, if one piece doesn't match the background, there's a chance that another will, so at least part of my human outline will be hidden. My outfit is usually completed by a decent pair of welly boots. Although they're not much good for stalking, wellies will keep your feet dry as you negotiate the varied, and often wet, terrain of an autumn wood in search of a suitable place to settle down and wait. As far as I'm concerned, it's worth spending a few pounds on a decent pair of wellies. Better quality boots have a much improved fit and don't slop around like the cheap ones, and they also tend to last much longer – like so many things in life, if you buy cheap, you usually end up buying twice.

The remainder of my kit comprises a few essentials that are stuffed into the pockets of my jacket. I always take a camouflage headnet and a pair of camo gloves to help keep me hidden. I like the thin gloves with the plastic stippling that improves grip, and I usually snip off the end of the right index finger so I can feel exactly what's happening when I take up the trigger. Last, but by no means least, one pocket will contain my sturdy hunting knife: an essential piece of equipment for tasks ranging from pruning branches to preparing shot quarry. On occasions when I will be hunting for more than two or three hours, I'll also take a backpack so I can carry a snack, something to drink and my photography kit. My camera and tripod are among the noisiest and most cumbersome pieces of kit that I take into the field. I'm pretty sure I'd shoot a lot more if I left them at home, but then nobody would be able to see what I get up to.

*The air rifle hunter can expect plenty of opportunities during the frenzy of activity in autumn woodland.*

Back to the hunt, you can expect squirrels, pigeons and corvids to be fairly active throughout the day at this time of year, but I don't think you can beat the first few hours after dawn or the period from mid-afternoon through to dusk. There's always a flurry of activity among wild creatures just after they awaken and just before they turn in for the night. Weather-wise, I prefer a fine day, mainly because it's a lot more pleasant, but also because the woodland residents seem to share my sentiments and also like to go about their business when it's dry and settled.

When I arrive at a familiar hunting ground, I've usually already got a hiding place in mind. Typically, it'll be among a stand of oak trees or beeches where I'd expect a wide variety of birds and animals to be attracted by the ripe, nutty feast. When I'm exploring a new patch of ground, I'll be looking for all the clues listed under the previous heading to point me in the right direction. Once I've identified the target area, my next consideration is to find a hiding place that provides good natural concealment from where I can cover a wide area while taking safe, unobstructed shots. Look into the treetops above and all around and consider how easy it will be to thread pellets through their stretching limbs when birds drop in or squirrels creep out. Beware of those thick clusters of fine twigs, they look frail and wispy but they'll act like an armour shield to anything behind, deflecting your humble airgun pellet way off course at the decisive moment.

Once I've located a promising area, I turn my attention to finding something to hide behind, or in front of. Although I prefer to get behind a tree trunk or amongst low, shrubby cover, it is possible to get away with little more than a backdrop of cover, especially once you've pulled on your headnet and gloves to hide your pink patches. Just make sure that the place you settle on is comfortable – as you may have to wait a while – and allows you to shoot from a relatively stable position.

More often than not, I'll choose to stand and wait, hiding behind the trunk of a tree. During your approach, you'll have noticed that the ground is covered in a layer of dry, crunchy leaves and twigs. This is especially so if there hasn't been any recent rainfall to soften the leaf litter. Moving about on a woodland floor like this is a noisy affair; even just shifting your weight from one foot to another is likely to make a din, which will soon be rumbled by the sensitive ears of your quarry. Luckily, the problem is easily remedied by simply shunting the leaves away with your foot until you're left with a soft, quiet carpet of dark, moist and delicious-smelling leaf mould. Clear a decent patch on the deck of your hiding place and you'll be able to shuffle around, moving to one side or another to get clear shots, without making a sound. Furthermore, the sweet aroma of composting leaves will probably help to mask your human scent.

Once you've settled in, there's nothing else to do but wait, and enjoy the peace and beauty of the autumn woodland. More than likely, the first arrivals will be songbirds. Listen for the watery warble of the nuthatch, for you're in his territory now, and look out for the little fawn treecreeper scuttling up the tree trunks and then flitting back down to begin his ascent again.

I've lost count of the times I've been completely absorbed in the antics of the woodland wildlife, only to have my attention yanked back to the job in hand by the noisy arrival of my quarry. Of all the raucous entrances, none can rival that of the jay. This colourful character usually makes its presence known long before it's visible. An eye-catching corvid, the jay has a surprisingly noisy call for such a small bird, and when you hear its prehistoric screech echoing through the woods, it's time to have your wits about you if you're going to stand any chance of bagging this wily customer.

Jays are very secretive and cunning birds that seldom venture far from the cover of the woods. Apart from the fact that they scarper at the least sign of danger, these crafty little corvids refuse to keep still for more than a moment at the best of times as they flit from branch to branch in a constant state of high alert. Their sheer cunning makes them a worthy adversary and their beautiful plumage makes them a glittering prize.

The jay is undeniably one of Britain's most beautiful birds: dressed in buff/pink plumage with a black and white crest, black-tipped wings and white rump. Most dazzling of all are its electric blue and black barred wing feathers. Apart from being a handsome prize for the hunter who manages to outwit such a cunning bird, the jay's wing feathers are cherished by fly tiers. The sparkling metallic blue and black plumage is used to create sea trout flies that imitate glistening

*A tree trunk is often all the cover that's required when woodland pests turn their attention to the autumn harvest.*

*Grey squirrels can be caught off guard when they're busy foraging nuts and acorns.*

fish fry. If you shoot a jay, don't waste its wings, cut them off and pass them on to a fly tier. Bag a few and you might even be able to earn a couple of pounds to put towards ammo.

As stunning as the jay looks, it is a close relative of the magpie and shares its bad habits. Although they like to feast on nuts and berries, jays are fully-fledged members of the corvid clan and love to eat the eggs and chicks of songbirds and game birds. Their nest-robbing antics have rightly earned these sharp-eyed corvids their pest status. They also share the amazing intelligence and cunning of the corvid family; if they catch just a glimpse of movement as you shoulder your rifle, they'll be gone before you even get to peep through the scope. You'll need to be on the ball, preferably with your gun shouldered and ready before this bird even flits into sight, if you're going to have any hope of adding one to the bag.

Less of a challenge than the ever-edgy jay are the plump autumn woodpigeons that swoop in to the stands of oaks and beeches before flapping down to the ground to scratch for beechmast or gorge on acorns. Although not as wary as corvids, pigeons have a healthy fear of anything out of the ordinary, so keep hidden and move slowly and quietly when chances come your way. I prefer to drop them from the treetops after they first fly in rather than waiting for them to alight on the ground. Pigeons waddle around all over the place, bobbing incessantly as they search for food among the fallen leaves, making it surprisingly tricky to compose a telling shot.

On my ground, grey squirrels provide the mainstay of autumn hunting trips in the woods. In fact, it is the need to control their numbers that motivates most landowners to grant me permission to shoot in the first place. At this time of year, you can expect to encounter an abundance of young squirrels, recently turned out from the drey and seeking territories of their own. These uneducated youngsters aren't usually as crafty as their parents, so now is a good time to make a serious start on your squirrel control campaign.

When controlling squirrels, the obvious places to target are close to any dreys that you manage to spot in the trees and, of course, any areas where the trees are heavy with the fruits and nuts that these bushy-tailed rodents like to eat. Squirrels should be very active through this season, and especially so towards the end of the day when the fading light seems to send them into a frenzy of activity before they bed down for the night. Keep a close eye on the treetops, but don't neglect the ground either. Grey squirrels spend a lot of time foraging among fallen leaves in search of tasty morsels that have dropped from the trees. They'll also be making scrapes to stockpile excess nuts for when pickings become lean. Squirrels are forgetful creatures and consequently lose track of many of their caches of nuts. This forgetfulness amounts to one of the few useful contributions made by grey squirrels, for their lost hoards help with the distribution and germination of seeds that will grow to form the next generation of trees. Unfortunately, if left unchecked, the resident population of bark-chewing squirrels will wreak untold damage on those new saplings as soon as they push through the ground.

The presence of birds of prey and corvids can sometimes force squirrels to reveal their hiding places. Grey squirrels are aggressive little animals and sometimes can't resist the urge to pop their heads up and abuse passing birds that you'd really expect them to be frightened of. So, whenever you see crows passing through, or perhaps a buzzard or little owl resting in a nearby tree, listen out for the scolding chatter of an angry squirrel.

Just a few weeks ago as I write, I witnessed the most courageous and foolhardy mobbing by squirrels that I've ever seen. I was hiding amongst a stand of ivy-clad oak trees, which appeared to be devoid of squirrels, when a buzzard swooped into one of the outer branches. Within seconds of the raptor landing, four squirrels appeared from nowhere and went bundling towards it. The assembled bushy-tails were making a heck of a racket, and one of the plucky little rodents ended up virtually face to face with the trespassing buzzard.

Confronted by a quartet of hissing squirrels, the old buzzard quickly realised that it was comprehensively outnumbered and flew off. The triumphant bushy-tails retreated back to their hiding places well before I could even think about taking a shot. In fact, I was so gobsmacked by what I'd just witnessed that I didn't even manage to get the gun to my shoulder. Looking back, I can only assume that the squirrels were confident that the buzzard presented no great threat as it wasn't in flight. Nevertheless, they took a big risk as squirrels are a regular feature on the buzzard's menu.

# Making use of fur and feather

Anyone who sets out to hunt live quarry with an air rifle should regard it as their duty to make the most of everything they shoot. When controlling pests such as rabbits and pigeons, the end use is obvious: these animals provide delicious free-range meat for the table, which is a great reward for time spent on crop protection duties. Finding

good uses for some of the other quarry species takes a little more thought, but there are a surprising number of people who would be more than grateful to get their hands on the fruits of a successful vermin control session – it's just a question of knowing who they are.

One group of avian pests that are highly unlikely to end up in the pot are the corvids. But, although I've yet to hear anyone raving about the culinary qualities of crows, magpies and jays, I know plenty of people who are very happy to take them off my hands.

The feathers of corvids are much sought after by trout fishermen who use them alongside other materials, such as tinsel, silk and fur, to make fly hooks. Fibres, particularly from the wing feathers, are whipped to fishing hooks to create eye-catching imitative flies, which they cast to hungry trout. When I can find the time, I enjoy a spot of trout fishing myself and, although I don't have the time, skill or inclination to tie my own flies, I have caught a trout with an imitation tied with materials from quarry shot with an airgun – more on that later.

When it comes to fly-tying materials, jays are the most revered members of the corvid clan. The black and electric blue wing feathers glisten in the water like the flanks of a small fish, and they're used to tie lures that anglers use to tempt elusive sea trout as they migrate back up the rivers to spawn.

But jays aren't the only corvids that fly-tiers will accept: feathers from crows and magpies are also gratefully received. The magpie's plumage may appear to be black and white to the casual observer but, when viewed up close, their wing and tail feathers reflect the iridescent blues and greens you would expect to see on a tropical bird. Similarly, crows' wings have a purple hue the fly-tiers use to imitate the glistening colours of insects' wings and the glossy sheen of beetles' shells.

So, before you dispose of the bodies of corvids after your pest control duties, snip off their wings. You'll need to snap

*The striking blue and black barred wing feathers of the jay are highly valued by fly-fishermen.*

the bone that locates to the shoulder and then trim off the wing with your hunting knife, or just clip through in one stroke with a pair of secateurs. I leave pairs of wings in my garden shed for a few days so they can dry out, and then bag them up and freeze them.

Although some people love to eat grey squirrel, I have to admit that I'm not one of them. When it comes to pigeons and bunnies, I can't wait to get shot quarry into the kitchen but, in my opinion, gutting and skinning a squirrel is a lot of work for a measly amount of meat, which is tougher and stringier than that of an old, over-wintered rabbit. Nonetheless, the meat from the squirrels I shoot doesn't go to waste. I have several friends who keep ferrets and are always grateful to receive some free meat to feed them. If you don't know any ferreters, your local wildlife rescue centre or falconry club might appreciate some squirrel meat to feed to their residents. That said, an increasing number of people are developing a taste for squirrel meat, so check with your local butcher or farm shop to see if they'd like to take them off your hands before you go giving them away.

And remember to use your hunting knife to cut off squirrels' tails at the base before you part with them. Store them in the way I suggested for corvids' wings and they'll have a similar use because their fibres are also used for fly-tying materials.

In terms of finding an outlet for fly-tying materials, think of friends, family members or work colleagues who like to fish for trout or salmon and ask them. Otherwise, get in touch with your local fly-fishing club. Alternatively, a simple online search will produce contact details for several fur and feather merchants who will be willing to pay for fly-tying materials. A pair of wings is only worth pennies, but I get enough to make a welcome contribution towards the cost of airgun pellets by storing wings in the freezer for a few months until I've accrued a decent batch to send by post.

Because I tend to sell my fur and feather via merchants, I don't get to see the end result. However, a few years ago my friend and fellow hunting writer Ian Barnett was kind enough to

*Squirrels' tails can be sold, as their fibres are used to tie imitation flies for trout fishing.*

*A trout caught on a fly tied with fibres from the tail of a grey squirrel.*

post me a trio of beautiful trout flies tied by an acquaintance of his using fibres from the tails of squirrels he'd shot. These fly hooks were skilfully tied in the pattern of nymphs and were well suited to one of my local fisheries. I vowed to bank a trout using one of Ian's squirrel-tail flies and, although it was a while before I found time to sneak out with rod rather than gun, I eventually succeeded in fooling a trout with one of them. As far as I'm concerned, the capture represented the end result of my two favourite pastimes, and was one of the most satisfying trout I've ever caught. And I'm pleased to say that the trout didn't go to waste and *did* end up on my plate.

# Hunting knife and sharpening

The subject of preparing fur and feather leads nicely on to that of knives, and I regard a decent hunting knife as an absolute essential. Mine is a stout, fixed-blade model that I use for all kinds of jobs from cutting off squirrels' tails and gutting rabbits to cutting sticks for makeshift hide poles and hacking back brambles along stalking routes. To be honest, it's a workhorse of a knife and, in terms of butchery, a bit too big for anything other than superficial game preparation. I tend to do my paunching in the field, leaving the guts behind for badgers and foxes to clear up. Then, when I get home, I use a smaller, much sharper knife to prepare shot game for the table. This little knife has a gleaming scalpel edge on it that's perfect for dressing shot quarry, but would get destroyed by the demands of a hunting trip.

I favour a simple fixed-blade hunting knife because this robust design stands up well to the sort of abuse I dish out in the field. I've got no time at all for the gimmicky multi-tool knives that seem to have been developed as the 'ideal' gift for the hunter who has everything. If you ask me, they're just a compromise between a proper knife and your toolbox at home. I don't expect to need a toolkit out in the field. If a screw works loose and falls out of your combo during the heat of the action, I would suggest that you go home, contact whoever supplied it to you and demand a refund because it should never happen. Similarly, I'm not a fan of survival knives that come complete with waterproof matches, fishing hooks and the like. While I always take safety precautions very seriously, a shooting trip is not the place to be playing soldiers. I would suggest that a

mobile phone provides better insurance against a 'survival' situation.

Because of the rough use my basic hunting knife gets in the field, it tends to lose its edge rather quickly, but this is soon remedied by a few strokes of the Blade-tech sharpener I carry on my key-ring.

I bought this compact sharpener at a game fair the best part of ten years ago and I've been really impressed with it. All you need is a flat surface to position it on – I've used everything from tree stumps to cattle troughs – and you're ready to go. I even use it to put an edge on my kitchen knives.

*A hunting knife needs to be a workhorse as it will be turned to a variety of tasks.*

*A compact knife sharpener enables the hunter to hone his blade in the field.*

*Lamping is a very effective means of controlling rabbits during the autumn months.*

# Lamping rabbits

For me, the harbingers of autumn – the dew-clad spiders' webs, the turning leaves and the shortening days – herald the start of my rabbit lamping season. It is perfectly legal to shoot rabbits by lamplight throughout the year, but there are several reasons why I rarely adopt this approach during spring and summer.

First and foremost, I lose my enthusiasm for night-time hunting during the warmer months because of the very obvious fact that it's so late by the time darkness has closed in. In midsummer, night doesn't fall until well after 10pm. By the time you've given the rabbits an hour or so to venture out, your foray wouldn't begin much before midnight so you wouldn't finish until nigh-on daybreak – I love my shooting, but not that much. Also, there is usually such an abundance of gullible young rabbits about during the middle part of the year that most reasonably competent hunters

should be able to outsmart a few for the pan without subjecting themselves to sleepless nights.

But the main reason why I tend to wait until autumn and winter before I reach for the lamp is because it is such an effective hunting tactic. Lamp rabbits hard during their peak breeding season and you risk wiping them out completely, leaving you with no meat to harvest later in the year. Although my summer pest control regime is pretty ruthless compared with that of many shooters, most of the landowners on my shooting permissions accept that a few rabbits will slip through the net. These farmers are content for the bunny population to be hammered down to an acceptable level rather than completely eradicated. Consequently, there are significantly less rabbits on these farms than if they were left uncontrolled, but pockets of rabbits remain to breed and recolonize.

Of course, there are situations where complete eradication is the ultimate aim: golf courses and equestrian holdings are examples that instantly spring to mind. If excavations carried out by burrowing rabbits are spoiling putting greens where club members pay good money for meticulous maintenance, or if a valuable or cherished horse faces the risk of a broken leg after a misplaced hoof ends up down a hole, there's hardly an excuse for taking a subtle approach. In these situations, a ruthless, round-the-clock campaign is likely to be called for; it's likely that you will have been called in as a pest controller and you'll have to live up to the title. Ultimately, the extent of the cull must be agreed between yourself and whoever has granted you permission to shoot. Speak with the person in charge and decide on the best approach for the job in hand, taking into account the constraints posed by other demands on your time, of course.

*A magazine-fed gun enables fuss-free reloading when hunting in darkness.*

As lamping is done under the cover of darkness, there's no need to worry about camouflage patterns. The latest designs of tree-print camo and all the manufacturers' marketing patter about how the stuff looks when viewed in an animal's colour spectrum make no difference at all when it's too dark to see (and arguably not much more in daylight). What does matter, though, is what your night-time hunting clobber sounds like. The single most important requirement for lamping attire (aside from hiding your nudity and keeping you warm) is that it should be as silent as possible. Sound seems to travel a lot further at night when there's much less ambient sound to mask your approach, and rattling zips or clomping boots will have rabbits running for cover long before you get within range.

When it comes to hearing just how noisy my hunting gear is, I follow the advice of the original air rifle hunter – the late, great John Darling. John suggested that shooters should wait up until the rest of the household has retired to bed and then slip into their hunting attire. Without the noise of the television, the radio and people talking or pottering about, the house falls deathly quiet and it is now that you'll be able to pick up on the sounds you wouldn't have otherwise noticed. In the silence of the night, you'll be able to hear just how much noise the poppers on your shooting jacket make when they knock together as well as the sound your trousers make as your legs brush against each other when you walk. Pop your car keys in your pocket and you're likely to be amazed by the racket they make. Listen for these telltale sounds and try to remedy them as far as reasonably possible before you venture out.

The other big concern is safety. It goes without saying that safety should always come first, and never more so than when shooting after dark. All kinds of untold hazards, such as steep slopes, ditches and machinery, lurk in the gloom, so make sure you are familiar with the layout of your shoot before trekking into the night. Some macho shooters scoff at those who carry a mobile phone in case of emergencies – but not me. Your mobile could save your life if you take a fall on the hills on a rough night. And it's just as important if you shoot with a buddy: I weigh around 14 stones and I can't imagine anyone would want to singlehandedly carry me two miles across the countryside if I happened to fall and break my leg!

It is also a wise move to let someone at home and the landowner know when you are going to

*The lamper's essentials, ready for action.*

be out and when you expect to return. That way, you'll be missed if you don't get home on time and your shoot owner won't panic if he sees lamplight beaming across the distant hills. The last thing you want is a worried landowner calling the police because they've spotted someone lurking in the dark. In fact, it's a very good idea to notify your local police station of your intended lamping session. It's a good way to ensure that they know what the situation is if they do happen to receive a report from someone who's noticed strange lights shining around the fields.

On the subject of lights, there is a bewildering array to choose from. The first choice to be made is whether to go for a hand-held lamp or one that clips onto your telescopic sight. Scope-mounted lamps are very handy pieces of kit, perfect for the lone hunter. Fitted via a mount that attaches to the tube of the scope, these nifty little lamps direct a spot of light wherever you point the gun. Apart from being great for rabbit shooting they're also very useful for nocturnal rat shooting forays. Opt for one with an adjustable mount so you can ensure that the beam aligns perfectly with your line of sight, and a quick-release attachment is also useful as you can snap it on and off as you need it, rather than feeling compelled to leave it fitted to your scope. Another very handy feature available on many gun lamps is a stock-mounted switch

which allows you to flick the light on and off without having to move your hands from the gun.

Hand-held lamps tend to provide a bigger and more powerful option when you have the luxury of a helper to do the lamping while you do the shooting. Most makes of both type of light are up to the job, but many of the more expensive ones are simply more lamp than any airgun shooter is ever likely to need. Unless you own a rimfire rifle and intend to also use your lamp for fox control, there's no need to splash out on a mega-powered torch. What is important is that it casts a decent beam of light a hundred or so metres, so you can use it for spotting rabbits out in the field before you stalk within range. Most importantly, the beam should be directed into a neat spot rather than having light spilling all over the place and even onto you. The simple fact is that lamps that spill light will attract unwanted attention from your quarry. Whether or not you opt for a lamp with a rechargeable battery is a matter of personal choice. Rechargeable battery packs are very convenient, but they do tend to be a little bulky – not that that's too much of a problem if you have the assistance of a lamp-man.

Many lamps can be fitted with filters to mute and change the colour of the beam. It is claimed that animals struggle to see light at the red end of the colour spectrum and shooters are often advised to use a red or amber filter when rabbits become lamp-shy after sustained shooting pressure. I'm not convinced and tend to think that filtered light is more inclined to go undetected simply because the brightness is reduced. Although I occasionally use red filters to dim down very bright lamps, I prefer to use a unit with adjustable power output. One thing I would stress is that I've rarely witnessed the often described phenomenon of rabbits sitting frozen to the spot after being dazzled by a super-powerful beam. In my experience, incredibly bright lights are more likely to send rabbits running for cover rather than pin them to the spot. I favour a lamp that is bright enough to do the job, but not so powerful that it causes alarm.

Other extras worth having with you on a lamping session include a decent-sized backpack. Shot rabbits are cumbersome and soon start to get heavy if you try to carry them by hand. A backpack spreads the load and keeps your hands free to do the shooting. Better still, hand over the bag to the lamp-man and you'll be able to shoot completely unhindered.

Weather conditions play a significant role in lamping success. In fact, they generally dictate whether or not I decide to head out at all. The ideal conditions are a really gloomy night with plenty of cloud cover. A breeze will also help to mask the sound of your approach and can be utilised to carry your human scent away from your quarry. A drop of light drizzle is no bad thing either, as the precipitation dampens down your odour as well as infusing the air with all kinds of natural smells that will help to keep yours hidden. Heavy rain usually sends rabbits to ground, and trying to lamp them on clear, still nights is a complete waste of time. On these cloudless nights, it just doesn't get dark enough to keep a hunter hidden. Add a full moon to the equation and you'll notice that you cast a shadow as if it were daytime; there's no way that rabbits will hang around while you trek around the fields in these conditions. Clear winter's nights also tend to coincide with still, frosty weather. Even a light touch of frost will turn a field of grass into a brittle mass of stems that crunch under every footfall. If clear skies and frosts are forecast, your time will be better spent at home in the warm.

When the weather is right and I decide to venture out, I bide my time rather than making a dash for the fields as soon as night falls. Hit the fields too early and the rabbits are unlikely to have had enough time to get right out and away from cover. Leave it until a couple of hours after nightfall and plenty of hungry bunnies should have ventured away from the cover of the hedgerows to where the thicker, richer grass grows. Given time to get further out in the fields, the rabbits will have to get past you to make it back to the safety of their burrows.

Once you're out in the field, keep as quiet as you can from the outset and try to plot a route around your shoot that keeps the wind in your face. As with any stalking, this will help to drift your scent and sound away from the quarry. Of course, you're highly unlikely to be able to stalk into the wind all of the time as you make your way around your permission. It makes for a useful rule of thumb, but safety, practicality and the general lie of the land means that you'll often have to compromise on this one.

Allow your eyes to adjust to the darkness and you'll be surprised by just how well you can see. Work your way steadily and stealthily around the field margins, with the lamp switched off, and stop from time to time to scan with the light.

*An extra pair of hands makes night-time shooting a lot easier – especially when there are obstacles to be crossed.*

Point the lamp at the ground in front of you as you switch it on and then begin to make slow, steady sweeps stretching gradually further from your position as you look for the telltale glow of light reflected from rabbits' eyes. The chances are that the first 'rabbits' you see will in fact be droplets of dew glistening in the lamplight. A rabbit's eye reflects a subtle amber hue compared with the clear glint of water droplets. Distinguishing them at range can be tricky in the early days, but it becomes easier with experience. After a few outings, you'll learn that if you think it's a rabbit it probably isn't – because when it *is* a rabbit you'll know.

Typically, the first proper sightings are usually out of range. At this point (when hunting with a lamp-man) we usually turn the lamp off and both creep to within about 50 or 60 metres of our quarry and then light-up again. All being well, the rabbits are still out grazing when the lamp goes back on. Now it's time for the lamp-man to keep still, holding the light on the target while the shooter stalks carefully along the outside of the lamp beam until he's within range. When hunting on my own with a scope-mounted lamp, I still usually switch off after the first sighting (because a moving lamp can spook rabbits) and then try to sneak all the way within range before switching back on and hopefully taking the shot.

Range estimation can be tricky at night. The hunter needs to be mindful that the gloom makes targets look further away than they actually are. Like most things, familiarity is the key.

When presented with a shot, I'll usually opt for the stability of a kneeling stance – even if the ground is wet and muddy. Freestanding shots are tricky at the best of times, and they're even harder when you've been yomping up and down hills in the dark, carrying a gun in your hands and a hefty deadweight of rabbits on your back. Allow your breathing to settle and take advantage of the extra support of the kneeling stance unless ground cover forces you to stand, in which case you may want to stalk closer than usual.

From time to time, when you shoot a rabbit by

*A backpack helps to keep hands free when carrying the night's haul.*

lamplight, one or two of its companions will hang around, presenting you with the opportunity to make another quick kill. A multi-shot rifle is a great advantage in this situation, enabling you to quickly breech another pellet without having to fumble around in the darkness.

As I've already suggested, a willing helper is a great asset when it comes to handling the lamp and carrying shot rabbits when the bag starts to swell. In all honesty, a bit of company is always welcome when I'm out at night on the windswept hills. A bit of banter is good for morale and it certainly makes it easier to drag yourself away from the comforts of home at a time when most people are just starting to settle down for the night. You and your lamp-man can even swap roles halfway round if you can both shoot accurately with the same combo.

An extra pair of hands is also most welcome when the time comes to paunch-out shot rabbits. Paunching is usually done at the end of the session, but it's sometimes necessary to lighten the load during a really productive night. It's surprising just how much ballast you can lose by gutting your haul. Above all, paunching in the field is a lot less hassle than tackling this messy but essential job at home. It also does away with waste disposal; guts should be left hidden among the undergrowth in some discreet place, although you can usually count on scavenging foxes and badgers to clear all evidence by sunrise.

Negotiating the countryside in darkness is a tiring business. You have to be aware of the placing of every footfall, especially if you don't want to come a cropper when it's slippery underfoot. On some farms, rabbit numbers will be so great that you could probably strike back out after completing a circuit of the holding, and find that plenty of rabbits have ventured out again. More likely, you'll have had your fill; your muscles will be aching and you'll be unable to resist the call of the snug bed that awaits you back at home.

# Recipes for autumn

## RABBIT AND MUSHROOM HOTPOT

Once you've confidently identified your mushrooms as eaters, this tasty dish combines the results of a successful autumn foray to create a wholesome meal that's perfect comfort food for when the nights start drawing in. It's certainly the recipe to turn to when you want something that's going to stick to your ribs.

For those of you who are more faint-hearted (or less reckless) in the kitchen, simply use mushrooms bought from the shop.

*To serve 4*

**Ingredients**

A knob of butter
1 tablespoon of olive oil
Best meat trimmed from the thighs and saddles of 2 full-grown rabbits, cut into chunks
About 225g of mushrooms (depending on how many you find), thickly sliced
900g of large potatoes, thinly sliced
2 large onions, sliced
3 or 4 sage leaves, chopped
2 sprigs of rosemary, chopped
570ml of chicken stock
Salt and pepper

Preheat the oven to 175°C, then heat the butter in a deep, flameproof casserole dish over the hob. Add the rabbit pieces and fry until lightly browned – this should take 3 or 4 minutes. Transfer the rabbit into a bowl, return the casserole dish to the heat, add the mushrooms and onions then stir-fry for 5 minutes or until soft. Stir in the herbs, remove from the heat and transfer to a separate bowl.

Layer half the sliced potatoes into the base of the casserole dish and season with salt and pepper. Cover with half the mushroom and onion mixture then top with rabbit pieces. Add another layer using the remaining mushroom and onion mixture and rabbit, then pour over the stock until just about covered. Cover with the remaining potato slices, brush with oil and season with salt and pepper.

Put the dish back on the heat until it reaches a gentle simmer. Cover and place in the oven for 1 hour. Remove the lid and return to the oven at 200°C for 30 minutes or until the top is brown. Serve with seasonal vegetables, and enjoy.

## PIGEON PASTIES

Pigeon breast is surprisingly similar to steak, so the meat works perfectly in this twist on the traditional Cornish pasty. I like them served with roasted parsnips, peas and gravy, though they're practically a pastry-packed meal so are just as good on their own.

This recipe makes three decent-sized pasties, so you'll be able to serve one each for yourself and your partner at dinner time and have one spare to stuff in your lunchbox next time you head out shooting.

**To make 3 large pasties, you will need:**

For the shortcrust pastry
Either buy ready-made shortcrust pastry from the shop or...
225g plain flour
110g butter
Pinch of salt
Glass of cold water

**For the filling**

Breast meat from 2 woodpigeons, cut into cubes
1 medium onion, finely diced
3 medium potatoes, finely diced
2 large carrots, finely diced
Half a medium swede, finely diced
Mixed herbs (fresh or dried)
Bottle of beer
1 beef stock cube
Knob of butter
Salt and pepper
Pinch of flour
1 egg

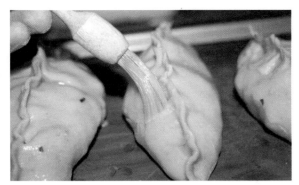

If you're making your own pastry, sift the flour and a pinch of salt into a large bowl. Cut the butter into small cubes and add. Use your fingertips to rub the butter into the flour until crumbly, but don't overwork the mixture. Add 1 tablespoon of water and use your hands to bring the mixture together into a pastry. Add another tablespoon of water if necessary, but don't make it too wet – it should bind cleanly and not be tacky. Place the finished pastry in a plastic bag and leave in the fridge for 30 minutes to chill.

Preheat the oven to 200°C. Cut the pigeon breasts into cubes and lightly flour. Peel and finely dice the onion, potatoes, carrot and swede. Chop the herbs.

Melt a knob of butter in a frying pan over the hob and brown the pigeon chunks. Remove from the heat and set aside.

Add the diced vegetables to the pan and cook, stirring occasionally, over a gentle heat for 5 minutes or until they begin to soften. Add a slosh (about a cupful) of the beer, sprinkle in the stock cube and chopped herbs and stir. Cook for another 5 minutes until the vegetables are soft and the beer has reduced to a stiff gravy and season to taste – if it looks a bit dry, add another slosh of beer. Remove from the heat and leave to cool.

Roll out the pastry to about 3mm thickness and, using a plate or bowl as a guide, cut out circles of around 20cm in diameter. Spoon a generous helping of the filling onto each circle. Brush the edges of pastry with beaten egg, bring the edges together and press firmly to crimp shut. Place the pasties on a greased baking sheet, brush all over with egg and cook in the oven for around 20 minutes or until golden.

## RABBIT WITH APPLE AND CIDER

This is a very tasty, and surprisingly quick, casserole that makes for a hearty dish at a time of year when rabbits and apples are abundant.

Being from Somerset, I'm always keen to incorporate farmhouse cider in recipes, but this fruity tipple really does work particularly well with rabbit. The caramelised apple topping gives it even more of a fruity lift, which is perfectly tempered by the tang of cider vinegar.

*To serve 4*

### Ingredients

Best meat from 2 rabbits, cut into chunks
1 handful of plain flour
Knob of butter
2 tablespoons sunflower oil
2 medium onions, sliced
225g mushrooms, roughly sliced
175g black pudding, sliced
275ml dry cider
1 tablespoon Worcestershire sauce
1 tablespoon light muscovado sugar
2 Cox's apples, cored, peeled and thickly sliced
1 tablespoon cider vinegar
Salt and pepper

Roll the rabbit in the flour until evenly coated and shake off any excess. Heat the oil in a casserole dish and cook the rabbit over a moderate heat, turning occasionally until golden brown, and then remove from the pan.

Add the onion to the pan and cook for 2 minutes, then add the mushrooms and cook for a further 2 minutes while stirring to prevent from sticking. Add the browned rabbit, black pudding, cider and Worcestershire sauce. Bring to the boil, cover and simmer gently for 1 hour, stirring occasionally, until the rabbit is tender. Season with salt and pepper to taste.

Melt the butter and sugar in a separate pan, then add the apples and cook gently for 2 or 3 minutes until golden. Sprinkle with the cider vinegar and allow to bubble for a few seconds. Spoon the apples over the casserole and serve hot, with crusty bread or roast potatoes and seasonal vegetables.

# WINTER

*Biting-cold winds, rock-hard frosts and flurries of snow may not be the sort of weather to tempt the average person away from the creature comforts of home and out into the woods, but the arrival of winter has hunters yearning for the great outdoors.*

*Dress appropriately and there's no need for inclement weather to leave you housebound at the time of year when the countryside can be at its most stunning.*
*Get yourself in the right place at the right time and you should also be in for some heart-warming action. The seasonal shortage of natural food results in high concentrations of quarry species in the places where they can find sustenance: be it squirrels stealing from pheasant feeders or rats raiding the farmyard.*

*Winter also brings excellent sport at the woodpigeon roost. And, with the days being so short, you should be able to make a decent bag of woodies and still get home in time for tea.*

# Pest control around pheasant feeders

If you thought the pheasant release pen attracted pests like a magnet in the autumn, just wait until there have been a few hard frosts. Scavenging squirrels, rats, magpies and corvids were happy to raid grain from the feeders earlier in the year because the easy pickings were a novelty, but they also had plenty of natural pickings to feed on. Now things are much tougher; nature's larder is all but bare and it's getting difficult to scratch any sustaining food from the frost-hardened ground. The pheasant feeders are a critical food source now – possibly the only food source.

Apart from the keeper's cherished pheasants, the feed hoppers could well be receiving visits from hundreds of other hungry mouths now that times are hard. As winter tightens its grip, the impact is considerable, and the uninvited diners will be munching their way through valuable feed. Grain is far from cheap and, as most shoots operate on tiny margins, it is a precious resource. If your shooting permission hinges on reducing numbers of grain-robbing pests in the woods, now is the time to be busy at it.

Although you can expect to encounter rats, magpies, jays and even the occasional woodpigeon tucking into the constant supply of grain provided by pheasant feeders, grey squirrels are usually the most frequent visitors. Squirrels are incredibly resourceful little critters so it doesn't take them long to tap into an easy food source, nor does it take them long to work out how to operate the mechanism that releases the corn at the base of the hopper.

Most people have witnessed how clever these greedy little rodents are by their ability to empty seemingly secure bird feeders in the garden. When presented with a problem, squirrels can usually be relied upon to find a solution if there's a food reward at the end, and they'll suss out the release system on a pheasant feeder in no time. Let's face

*Squirrels quickly learn that pheasant feeders offer an easy meal when natural food is scarce.*

it, if a dopey chicken-brained pheasant can operate one of these things it's hardly going to present much of a challenge to a cunning squirrel that's used to living on its instincts.

Apart from costing gamekeepers or their employers dearly in terms of wasted grain, the grey squirrel's habit of raiding hoppers causes numerous other problems. There's the obvious nuisance of extra trips to keep feeders filled so they can do their intended job of nourishing the resident pheasant population despite having their contents decimated by countless greedy squirrels. Some feeders will inevitably be situated in remote locations far from the beaten track, and the last thing the keeper wants is to have to make additional visits, either lugging grain by hand or by burning valuable fuel in the quad bike, because his birds are forced to share their meals with thieving rodents. Equally important, though, is the fact that the raids will be helping to sustain an unwanted population of grey squirrels.

In the absence of game feed, the harsh realities of winter should help to curb squirrel numbers as there would inevitably be casualties to starvation during prolonged periods of punishing weather; that doesn't happen when their meagre winter diet is being supplemented by a calorie-rich feast of corn. And, as well as helping more individuals to survive the ravages of winter, those that do will be in rude health as a result. Whereas most wild creatures emerge from the grips of winter in relatively poor condition after using all of their precious reserves simply to survive, corn-fed squirrels will be big and strong, thanks to their supplementary diet. As spring gradually revives the natural world from the torpor of winter, this inflated population of well-nourished bushy-tails will be ready to wreak their usual havoc. Warming rays of sunshine will kick-start the trees back into life, prompting them to produce tender buds and sending the sap coursing back through their cells. The squirrels know this and they'll be using their sharp incisors to strip back the bark so they can lap at the sweet, syrupy liquor that flows beneath. The result is dead or deformed trees and furious foresters.

For the gamekeeper who lost goodness knows how much grain to squirrels, more anguish is still to come. The legions of squirrels he inadvertently fed through the colder months will be on the hunt for eggs just as his overwintered pheasants and partridges begin to lay their precious clutches. Eggs and young of the helpless songbirds, which somehow managed to survive the frost and snow, are equally vulnerable.

But it's not all bad news. The appeal of pheasant feeders means we hunters know where to expect the squirrels to be during the winter. Also, the unseasonal abundance of food tends to make them rather cocky, and I certainly think that grain-raiding squirrels are a lot bolder than those that have to scratch a living from natural reserves. This is vital intelligence for the airgun shooter, who not only stands a very good chance of pinpointing this pest when the weather turns cold, but can also expect his quarry to be a little less wary than usual.

When it comes to picking my time for controlling squirrels around feed hoppers, I

*Sit and wait, and shots will soon be presented when squirrels scamper down to raid grain hoppers.*

usually opt for the first couple of hours after daybreak or the last few hours before nightfall. The reason these times tend to be the most productive is fairly obvious: at this time of year, the nights are very long; squirrels are not nocturnal so they'll be curled up asleep for as long as 16 hours. When they wake up from an extended slumber like that, they're going to be hungry, so you can expect them to head out in search of grain pretty soon after sunrise. Similarly, they usually become very active towards the end of the day, when they'll be busy filling their bellies in readiness for another long snooze.

The weather can also greatly influence the behaviour of grey squirrels. The belief that these animals hibernate is a common misconception – they don't. However, it does appear that they will remain in their dreys for several days at a time (either sleeping or just keeping warm) if conditions turn really foul. By and large, though, squirrels don't mind the cold and I've shot plenty on days when the mercury has refused to rise above zero. One thing squirrels really don't like is wet weather. I don't recall ever having any great success with them on a rainy day, and I'm reliably informed by a forester friend who is also a great naturalist, that squirrels are more likely to perish as a result of getting soaked than from exposure to extreme cold. That suits me fine as I'd much rather head out on a cold day than one that brings the threat of heavy downpours.

So, I favour a cold, crisp day for targeting grain-robbing squirrels. Ideal conditions would be a frosty morning after the sort of night that leaves the ground too hard for squirrels to scratch out the nuts and seeds they stashed underground back in the autumn. A blue sky with some weak rays of winter sunshine to help lull the squirrels from their beds would be just about perfect, along with a gentle breeze that's just strong enough to create a little noise and movement to help keep a hunter hidden, but not so strong as to stifle the sound of an approaching squirrel. Of course, it's usually a compromise in the real world where busy hunters with jobs and families head to the woods when they can, not when they'd like to, but there's no harm in hoping.

Rather than trying to stalk within range of squirrels, the best tactic is to set up an ambush. That said, feed hoppers should always be approached with stealth because you may just be rewarded with the chance of a shot when you arrive. Sometimes you'll encounter a squirrel or two feeding contentedly, sometimes you'll be rumbled and just catch a glimpse of the bobbing tail of a departing squirrel, and sometimes you'll see no sign whatsoever. An actual sighting is an obvious clue and such places are worth devoting some time to. If, however, you don't see any squirrels around the feeders when you visit, look for other signs to point you in the right direction. The hoppers worth targeting are the ones situated among squirrelly habitat: places with stands of ancient knurled oak trees that are full of hollows and other hidey-holes, places where mature trees are clad in the sort of dense ivy that provides shelter for squirrels, and places where you've spotted dreys nestled in the cleft between tree trunk and bough. If there are squirrels in the vicinity, you can expect the feeders to be receiving visits. Remember to have a good look around the hoppers too. Make sure they've got grain in them, because if they're not being regularly filled the squirrels will turn their attentions to the ones that are. You will sometimes find more clues under the feeders. Are there footprints in the damp soil and are there any rat holes worth keeping an eye on while you sit in wait?

When you find a feeder or group of feeders that warrant targeting, you'll need to get yourself in the right place. Having identified the places you expect to hold squirrels, you want to ensure that you'll be able to cover the bushy-tails as they advance from their hiding places towards the food source. Most importantly of all, you'll need to be able to see the feeder/s, and you'll need to be able to take safe, unobstructed shots at the squirrels when they reach them.

Because the squirrels will be distracted by the urge to feed, they'll probably be less wary than usual. Although this can change once they've been subjected to some shooting pressure, you're unlikely to need to construct a proper hide during the early stages of your campaign. My typical approach is to wear full camouflage and settle myself amongst whatever natural cover I can find. Disappearing into the countryside in this way is usually far less conspicuous than creating a new structure in the shape of a hide or blind that could well draw attention towards you. The trick is to make yourself comfortable in a place that offers

you a steady shooting position where you'll be able to sit for a couple of hours without getting cramps. I always keep a plastic bag in my shooting jacket so that I can clear a spot among the soft, spongy leaf-mould and then set it down to create a dry place to sit. Slip a beanbag shooting seat into your backpack and you'll be able to sit in real comfort, and the insulation provided by the polystyrene balls will help to prevent you from getting a cold backside. Bearing in mind that it could well be a seriously cold day, make sure that you're dressed for the weather. Put on plenty of layers and remember that a hat and gloves will help to keep you concealed as well as warm. An extra pair of socks will also keep the cold from setting in and buy you some extra time before you're forced to creep off home in search of warmth, when you should be out teaching the grey squirrels a lesson. On bitterly cold days, I'll also stow a flask of tea in my backpack so I can enjoy a piping hot drink and keep the cold from setting in. Stay warm and comfortable and you'll make good decisions and shoot well; let the weather get the better of you and things won't go so well. Winter shooting can be tough, and you won't perform to anything like the best of your ability if you're shivering – nor will you want to.

Once you've got yourself in position, perhaps at the base of a thick tree trunk or among the evergreen cover provided by holly, laurel, yew, rhododendron or wild privet, keep your eyes and ears peeled because squirrels can appear at any time.

Small birds are usually the first diners to arrive at the feeder,

*These three greedy squirrels fell for the lure of grain put out for pheasants.*

often followed by pheasants. Woods managed for game are a haven for wild birds because people like you and me reduce predation by keeping numbers of crows, magpies and grey squirrels in check, and also because gamekeepers put out so much grain. While keepers may not tolerate thefts of corn by pest species, most take pride in the fact that their work helps fragile populations of wild birds to flourish. Because of this, you can expect to be entertained by robins, sparrows, chaffinches and sometimes more unusual visitors as you keep watch over the hoppers.

Often, it's the burst of tiny wings that alerts the shooter to the arrival of a squirrel. Startled finches will often flutter away when a hungry bushy-tail comes bounding towards the grain. At other times, you'll see the telltale sign of a wavering branch as an acrobatic squirrel bounces along a springy limb, or perhaps you'll hear the subtle click of fine claws against bark as Nutkin scrabbles down a tree trunk. You need to keep your wits about you, tune into the sounds of the woodland environment and listen for clues. Remember also to scan the trees carefully, squirrels have a habit of sitting silently, huddled in the cleft where a branch forks out from the main trunk.

If I spot a squirrel on the move, I try to follow it through the scope until it presents a clear, safe shot within range. Fidgety squirrels can be infuriating, but will usually stop if you startle them by clicking your tongue or by making a squeaking sound through pursed lips. This ruse usually works, causing your quarry to freeze as it tries to locate the source of the sound, although there are times when it just sends jittery squirrels running for cover. The hunter must learn to sit tight and avoid taking hurried shots. By being patient you may miss the occasional opportunity, but you can rest assured that the lure of the grain is likely to mean you'll soon be presented with another. Above all, resist the urge to take shots that pose any risk of damaging the gamekeeper's feeders. You'll struggle to justify the impression you're making on pest numbers if you put holes in the equipment while you're at it.

# Hide shooting for hungry crows

Observant readers will notice a pattern emerging here, and that is that one of the most reliable ways to outwit wary pests is to catch them when they're trying to fill their bellies. This applies even more in the winter when food supplies are scarce and hunger is compounded by the cold, and even wily old crows can fall for a free meal at this time of year.

The baiting techniques I'm about to explain build on the methods described for building a fake nest in the spring or for capitalising on combine casualties in the autumn. The following tactics will work throughout the year, but they're even more effective in the winter because crows become ravenous during prolonged spells of cold weather.

The options for potential baits are considerable. In fact, it's probably fair to say that the only limitation is your imagination. Carrion is a favourite snack of the corvid clan. It's where the name carrion crow hails from and it's why crows like to lurk around sheep during lambing time. Most people will have witnessed corvids scavenging dead meat in the shape of road kill; look out for splatted rabbits and badgers when you're out in your car and you can bet that crows and magpies will be in the vicinity, especially if the road is a quiet one.

In keeping with their fondness for meat, the classic bait for attracting hungry crows is a rabbit with a cut made along its belly to reveal its intestines. Give the bunny a shake so its guts really hang out and it'll have even more appeal; it may not be a method for shooters with weak stomachs but trust me, crows regard offal as something of a delicacy. Lay out the disembowelled bunny with its belly pointing skywards and you should soon have scavenging crows circling overhead like vultures. If the scene looks safe, they'll soon drift down for a closer inspection.

*A dead rabbit and crow decoy will often tempt corvids when cold weather has given them a hunger.*

on soil that has recently been ploughed, where it stands out like a beacon to passing crows.

Because crows have adapted to take advantage of man's wastefulness by scavenging around bin bags and rubbish dumps, you can even draw them in by recreating your own pile of garbage. This is particularly effective on ground close to urban areas where trash makes up a large part of the crows' diet. One of my shoots is close to a landfill site, and I've used piles of leftover chips and potato peelings, complete with scrunched-up newspaper and crisp packets, to lure opportunistic corvids within range.

I try to keep one or two rabbits (with their guts left in and skins left on) in the freezer ready to be defrosted for crow shooting sessions, although a dead squirrel will also do the trick. I also know of shooters who bag up and freeze the guts of paunched rabbits and use this for bait; it's a wise way to make use of the by-product of a successful rabbit shoot.

If you're squeamish, not allowed to keep corpses in the kitchen freezer or simply don't want to get your hands dirty, there are several less offensive baits that can still be effective: bread being one of the most obvious ones. Like many birds, crows recognise bread as food and take it freely – probably because they're accustomed to encountering it on the bird table or finding discarded crusts thrown out with the rubbish or flicked out of the car window onto grass verges. Whatever the reason, crows know that bread equals nutrition and they'll swoop down to pick up pieces if there's no obvious danger lurking. I've had great results using white bread ripped into large chunks and scattered around a likely spot. It works best on dark ground, particularly

Whatever bait you opt for, results will be best if you target an area that is already receiving attention from scavenging crows: maybe corvids are making a nuisance of themselves by raiding animal feed from the farmyard, in which case you could set up your ambush in an adjacent field, or perhaps they're flocking to the edges of the woods where the pheasant feeders are sited, or maybe they've been attracted by sheep out on open ground.

After identifying a potentially productive area and deciding on your choice of bait, the next job is to identify a suitable site to construct a hide. Bearing in mind how sharp-eyed crows are, even when they're distracted by the allure of a free meal, I almost always opt for a net hide for this type of shooting. Ideally, I'll be looking for a site where it will discreetly blend in with the existing landscape, so it will usually be situated along the hedgerow or woven amongst a bush. At this time of year, the hedgerows are usually very bare so try to find a place that provides an effective backdrop to prevent you from being silhouetted from behind. Sometimes the cover is dense enough to

*Wrap up warm for an early morning ambush and you'll be able to shoot to your full potential.*

achieve this, and better still if you can set up with a bank behind you to provide a totally solid backdrop. Frequently, there just won't be enough cover behind you to stop telltale chinks of light from spilling through and betraying your presence when you make even the slightest movement. This situation is easily fixed by draping some dark hide netting behind you to screen off any unwanted gaps; if backlighting is a real problem you can even fold up the netting to make it twice as thick.

With the backdrop taken care of, it's time for the usual hide building process or clearing the ground to create a comfortable space to sit and shoot without getting tangled in brambles or impaled on thorns. If you can't drape your main hide net from the branches of hedgerow shrubs or fencing, use proper hide poles or hazel sticks to create a frame that provides just enough space without being cramped: you don't want to end up squashed inside a tiny hide but nor do you want it to be any bigger or more conspicuous than necessary. Drape the netting in place to create not only a screen around the front and sides, but also a roof over the top. You need to create a complete shell to keep hidden from these fickle corvids, and the open-topped hide arrangement used by shotgunners to target woodies will not suffice; if the crows get a glimpse of you they'll push off. And remember to peg down the bottom edges of the net, either with metal pegs or sticks if there's any hint of a breeze. The pegs will stop the net from flapping and can also be used to pin it away from you, thus creating a bit more space in the hide.

Hide dressing is more important than ever at this time of year. You need to weave natural material into the netting to soften its appearance and blur it into the landscape, but you also have to be careful not to create a stack of green foliage that stands out like a sore thumb against the muted browns and greys of the winter countryside. The field margins should contain just what you want, and an armful of dried-out cow parsley and nettle stems is probably all you'll need to make the netting disappear. As ever, make sure you arrange the vegetation so it looks like it grew there; crows will quickly spot signs like upside-down leaves and horizontal stems, and will shun anything that looks unnatural.

As cunning as crows are, they're not very good at counting. Indeed, this premise forms the basis of the old gamekeepers' ruse of setting out a bait and getting two people to walk nonchalantly to a hide in full view of the crows, then getting one to walk back equally nonchalantly. The crows assume that the danger has passed when the extra man leaves and then, if all goes to plan, fly in to investigate the bait where the remaining shooter is waiting in the hide ready to give them a pasting. Although I've never actually tried this tactic, I frequently use a variation of it because it is apparent that crows will often keep a safe distance from a hide for a while after you've built it. I imagine this is mainly because of the disturbance caused to passing birds while you've been busy constructing your camouflaged cocoon. What I try to do to remedy this is build my hide a day or two before I plan to use it. I then leave the site in the hope that some of the crows will see me going and feel that the threat has gone in the same way they do when the first man leaves the hide as previously described. Of course, that leaves my hide empty, so I then set my alarm early so I can return before sunrise, lay out my bait and sneak back into the hide under the cover of darkness without the crows knowing.

I still get as excited about my shooting now as I did when I was a teenager some two decades ago, and the anticipation of a good session at the crows can literally give me a sleepless night. That said, I always manage to slip off at some point and it's never easy dragging myself from the warmth of my bed when I know the temperature outside is below zero.

It's at times like this that the importance of careful preparation is drummed home. I make sure everything is done the night before: rabbit defrosted, clothes laid out, sandwiches made and flask out ready to be filled, so I can do the final preparations on autopilot before I stumble out into the freezing air.

Once I'm out in the open, my enthusiasm fizzes right back up because few things rival the exhilaration of being out in the wild when the rest of the world is asleep. You'll be yomping across the fields in a silent world where the only sound is your feet crunching down on grass that's brittle with frost, and your sight doesn't extend far beyond the steaming breath that's billowing from your mouth and nostrils. The cold is a factor that mustn't be underestimated, so

*The promise of a free breakfast proved irresistible to these corvids.*

remember to wear plenty of layers, put on that extra pair of socks and pack the flask of hot tea. Let the cold winter air get the better of you and you'll quickly get frustrated and despondent, and the advantage of that early rise will have been wasted as you give in to the call of the central heating and head home before the session has had a proper chance to unfold.

When you get to your hide, pace out whatever range you feel confident to shoot over – usually somewhere between 20 and 30 metres – and set out whichever bait you've chosen where it will be in clear view of the hide, and unobstructed by twigs or stalks. Whatever bait option you go for, one or two decoys will help to draw it to the attention of passing corvids. As well as highlighting the bait, the imitation birds create the illusion of a safe place to feed and give the impression of competition that should make passing corvids even more eager to get in quick before it's all gone. Crow and magpie decoys should both work, and I use all sorts of variations: a single crow or magpie, one of each or a matching pair. Recently, I've had some good bags of crows drawn down to bait by a pair of magpie decoys. As described in the chapter on pigeon decoying in the 'Summer'

section, a shot bird propped up with a short piece of wire pushed through its chin can make for a very attractive decoy. It stands to reason that a dead crow or magpie will look more convincing than a plastic replica.

With the trap set, crawl back into your hide and make yourself comfortable before the corvids set out on their early morning rounds at daybreak. These birds are notoriously wary and you may well need more camouflage than just the hide to keep you entirely hidden. Owing to the cold it's likely that you'll be wearing a hat anyway. If so, opt for a peaked one to cast some shadow over your face, or go the whole hog and wear a headnet. Gloves will also serve the dual purpose of protecting your fingers from the chilly air and preventing a flash of pink from betraying your presence when you move to take a shot.

When the first bird of the session swoops down to scrutinise the bait, slide the barrel of your airgun through the hide netting, slowly and gently – you don't want to catch the eye of your quarry by shaking the screen. Make sure the muzzle is pushed well clear of the netting and beyond any of the material you used to dress the hide. Trust me, the last thing you want to do is go to all the trouble of building a hide and getting up early for a dawn ambush only to fluff the first chance of the session by settling the crosshairs on a crow's head, touching off the trigger and firing a shot into a stem that was out of focus and out of sight. I've done it on more than one occasion and, with nobody to blame but yourself, it's the sort of mistake that leaves you wanting to chew your hide poles …

As with most hunting situations, there will be days when your efforts are wasted and the birds refuse to play. But, more often than not, this method works and you'll be rewarded with shots. On a really good morning, you may have to break cover from time to time to clear up the shot birds or replace your decoys with them. However the morning unfolds, you can be certain that you'll be ready for a hearty breakfast by the time you've packed up your gear and trudged back across the fields.

# The winter crow roost

Crows are notoriously wary of man. Sharp of eye and keen of ear, they are adept at detecting danger and treat virtually everything with suspicion. Although they are largely solitary birds, crows often gather in large numbers to roost during the colder months. They're also a little less cautious at the end of the day when their thoughts turn to bedding down for the night. For this reason, locating the whereabouts of the roost can be very useful if crow numbers need to be reduced around the woods where you shoot.

Just as they're often the earliest risers, crows are usually the last of the birds to go to roost, often staying away from the woods for some time after the pigeons have stopped flighting to their roosts. So, if you're going to shoot crows at roosting time, you'll have to stay in the woods until long after the sun starts to sink behind the hills. You can use the crows' late roosting habits to your advantage, whiling away the early part of the evening targeting pigeons for the pot before heading to the crows' roost for some serious pest control.

Because of their liking for late nights, roost shooting for crows means you'll be in the woods during a magical and mysterious time. It's an exciting and sometimes nerve-wracking experience being alone, miles from civilisation, surrounded by trees and enclosed in a veil of darkness at a time when most people are tucked up in the comfort of their homes. You'd expect the woodland to become silent as its inhabitants settle down to sleep, but the daytime animals are replaced by nocturnal creatures and, although ambient sounds such as traffic and the wind usually drop to the merest whisper, the wildlife can be quite noisy. The silence is frequently shattered by the screech of an owl, the cry of a vixen and the heavy shuffling of a badger among the dry leaves of the woodland floor. If you let your imagination get the better of you, it's quite easy to get spooked, but keep level-headed and it's a truly wild experience to savour.

If you share your ground with pheasant shooters, you can expect the late evening cull to score some major points with your host because the crow's nest-robbing habits have a serious impact on coveted wild broods of these ground-nesting game birds. From your own point of view, you can also take pride in the fact that you'll be leaving a few less of these opportunist predators to wreak havoc when the songbirds start to nest in early spring.

The best way to locate an active crows' roost is to wait in the woods until the fading rays of sun are replaced by moonlight. As night starts to fall, look upwards in search of the dark silhouettes drifting against the purple glow of the sky. If you fail to see them, you'll probably hear them because crows become quite vocal before they huddle down to sleep. It is also possible to find signs of a busy crows' roost during the daytime. Crows like a good vantage point from which they can survey the surrounding countryside, so concentrate on the areas with the loftiest trees. If the leaf litter below is splashed with watery white droppings, it's likely that you've found what you're looking for.

*Shade provides vital concealment when targeting crows in sparse winter woodland.*

Closer inspection will probably reveal one or two black feathers dotted about on the ground.

I like to arrive at the roost just before sunset so I can get myself hidden in some discreet place before the crows start to drift in, so don't milk the tail end of the pigeon roost for too long if you intend to move on in pursuit of crows. Turn up too late and you risk disturbing early arrivals: crows that have been frightened away by a clumsy hunter tend to be extra cautious when they return and their edgy behaviour will make the rest of the flock suspicious. The last thing you want to do is put these tricky customers on high alert.

As with so many hunting scenarios, I begin by trying to find the most suitable ambush point. Because crows like to scrutinise their surroundings from the tallest trees before they settle among the lower limbs, these are the ones I want to be able to cover from my hiding place. The best trees to shoot them from are the ones with open branches that will present clear silhouette shots when the crows pitch in – mature ash trees usually have a nice open form. It doesn't take much to knock a humble airgun pellet off its course. Make the mistake of positioning yourself in a place that puts a haze of wispy twigs between you and the birds, and you'll be ripping your hair out as the fine branches deflect shot after shot well wide of the mark.

I rarely build a full hide for this sort of ambush because the disturbance can often be more than the birds will tolerate. When crows are extremely cautious, perhaps after prolonged and intensive shooting pressure, it can occasionally pay to build a more substantial, permanent hide. In this situation, I'll construct a screen from dead branches and leave it for the birds to become accustomed to. However, I usually opt for a more mobile approach. Words fail to describe the frustration you'll feel after going to the trouble of building what looks like the perfect permanent hide only to discover that it would have been far more effective a few feet to one side or the other once the crows come in to roost!

The best way to avoid making incoming crows suspicious is to make the absolute most of natural cover rather than making your own. Tangles of fallen branches, dense undergrowth and even something as simple as a tree trunk can be all it takes to hide your human form from prying eyes – especially if you dress from head to toe in camouflage. If existing cover looks too sparse, lean a couple more branches into the arrangement to add to the break-up effect. The fading light will help with your concealment, but keep your face well hidden because crows will back away from anything that suggests the presence of a human. Illuminated by the gentle glow of the evening sky, your face and eyes stand out far more than you'd imagine as you stare up from the gloom of the twilit wood. Wearing a headnet can feel like a bit of an encumbrance, but it's the best solution to this problem.

Once in position, it's the usual routine of waiting quietly and tuning into the woodland sounds. The chattering calls of the migratory fieldfares will often be replaced by the cries of the awakening tawny owls before you hear the first croak of an incoming crow. You'll also sometimes get chances at grey squirrels while you're waiting for the corvids to come to roost. It's well worth taking advantage of these extra pest control opportunities as the bushy-tails busy themselves before they retire to their beds, but remember to make sure, as ever, that all shots are safe. Low shots shouldn't be taken unless you're confident that your pellet will terminate at a safe backstop: simply shooting into the blackness and expecting twigs and branches to catch the shot is far too reckless and carries an unacceptable risk.

When the crows do arrive they usually start to show in ones and twos. These early scouts usually pass high overhead, croaking to each other and scanning for any sign of danger before they commit to landing on a high treetop for a closer inspection. A crow caller can sometimes be used to coax these birds in. I occasionally give the caller a few blows, mimicking the calls of the crows, to lure them closer. However, this method doesn't always work and can sometimes make incoming birds even more suspicious, so I advise

*Used sparingly, a crow caller can help to pull incoming birds in your direction.*

The silenced muzzle report of an air rifle means you should be able to nail a few crows before their flock mates become suspicious. Even if the crows spot one of their comrades being downed, it doesn't necessarily mean they'll shy away. In fact, they frequently do quite the opposite.

In any crow-shooting situation, you need to be prepared to capitalise on the frenzy that can be provoked by killing one of their number. Common sense dictates that most wild creatures tend to shy away after witnessing the death of a companion, but crows don't always subscribe to that theory. Instead, they sometimes go into a loud frenzy, literally hurling themselves into the scene of the danger. It all happens very quickly: one moment you'll be congratulating yourself on plopping a crow from its lofty perch, and the next thing you know the sky is filled with the silhouettes of large birds swooping overhead. It can become quite unnerving, scary even, as dozens of agitated crows shriek and squawk as they circle the treetops above you. But stay calm and watch them carefully because one will soon make the mistake of gliding down so it can continue to croak and screech from the uppermost branches of a nearby tree. Through your scope, you'll see the frantic bird peering down into the darkness in search of the unlucky one. Hold your nerve, and shoot calmly, and you should be able to flop one or two more down into the leaf litter. Carefully mark the places where they fall so you can retrieve them by torchlight when the activity dies down.

putting the caller away if you fail to draw a bird in after giving it a couple of blasts.

If you're in the right place, the chances are you'll soon be presented with a shot. More often than not, a scope with a conventional reticule will be up to the task of shooting at dusk. The dark form of a crow stands out surprisingly well as long as you set up in a place that will present targets that are silhouetted against the sky, which should still be quite light with the afterglow of the sinking sun. Remember also to wind down the magnification of your scope a little lower than your usual daytime setting: this enables the lenses to transmit more light and results in a brighter sight picture. Occasionally, however, you'll struggle with your crosshairs becoming lost against the black of the crow and the branches behind it. A scope with an illuminated reticule is excellent in these conditions. You don't want to light up the reticule too bright or it'll spoil your natural night vision: set it so there's just enough of a glow to stand out against the background. Manufacturers offer a wide selection of scopes with reticules that light up either red or green. In my experience, colour choice makes no apparent difference.

Whether or not the crows decide to fling themselves into this strange funeral ritual, which momentarily robs them of their usually high sense of self-preservation, you can expect more opportunities to arise as the remaining glow of sunset fades to darkness. There's often a flurry of action just before it gets too dark to shoot. More and more birds will wheel overhead, and don't be surprised to see groups of jackdaws flighting along with the crows. Like the rest of the corvids, magpies also like to stay up late, so listen out for their chattering among the

*Linger in the winter woods until nightfall and you can expect to encounter more than just crows.*

shrill call of the crows. If you do hear magpies coming, be prepared to make a swift shot. These black and white bandits tend to bumble through the woods, bouncing from tree to tree and only lingering very briefly, as they make their way to the sheltered spot where they roost: often in the thickest tangle of overgrown blackthorn.

The twilight corvid cull can be lonely, cold and sometimes creepy, but there are ample rewards for the shooter who lingers in the winter woods after the sun goes down. A mixed bag is always on the cards and it's an effective way of thinning out crows and magpies before their nest-robbing habits impact on populations of less aggressive birds in the spring.

## Woodpigeons at the roost

Roost shooting for woodpigeons is one of the highlights of my shooting year. Pigeons are recognised as a serious agricultural pest and farmers know all too well that large flocks of these birds can decimate acres of crops in no time.

This plump bird also happens to taste delicious: the breast meat in particular is firm, dark and full of flavour. So, as well as contributing towards your pest control efforts, chilly evenings spent in the woods will also be rewarded with some fine wild meat that's perfect for all sorts of mouth-watering winter recipes.

When the harsh weather of winter has stripped the trees of their leaves, vast flocks of woodpigeons gather to roost in sheltered patches of woodland. This is a time of wonderful opportunity for the stealthy air-gunner who's prepared to wrap up against the elements and lurk amongst the trees as the sun sets over the woods. Woodland shooting can be both enjoyable and productive in the warmer months, but it's a lot trickier (especially in the low light levels of roosting time) because it's so much harder to see and shoot through the foliage. My urge to get out and do any kind of shooting increases dramatically when the days are shorter and there's a nip in the air. Yes, I sometimes come home with numb toes and throbbing cold fingers, but I always think it's worth the bother when I'm sat warming up in front of the fire with a bowl of steaming pigeon broth at the end of the night.

*Winter roost shooting for woodpigeons can provide the airgun shooter with great sport, and meat for the pot.*

Obviously, the culinary pay-off depends on bagging one or two woodies for the pot, and it's no secret that woodland hunting in winter can be just as thankless, and downright soul destroying, as it is in the summer when things don't go to plan; only it's worse because you come home cold as well as empty-handed. However, get it right and it really is an experience to savour.

The good news is that, although it doesn't always yield such big bags, roost shooting is usually a more reliable way of shooting pigeons than decoying – and it takes a heck of a lot less effort in terms of equipment and preparation. The main advantage of roost shooting can be attributed to the habitual nature of pigeons when it comes to bedding down for the night. During times of cold and rough weather, these birds gather in large flocks and tend to favour particular roosting sites. So, you can usually expect continually productive sessions from the same area of woodland once you locate their favourite place to roost. The same cannot be said for decoying over arable land, as pigeons often change their feeding sites at the drop of a hat – usually after you've gone to the trouble of building a fancy hide! Be mindful not to subject a productive pigeon roost to relentless shooting pressure, though, overshoot a roost and the remaining woodies will move on elsewhere.

Locating a roosting site isn't difficult as there are usually plenty of signs to guide the inquisitive hunter who's prepared to turn detective. The most obvious clue is a splattering of thick white droppings on the woodland floor. Find this and it's likely that you've found a place where pigeons like to gather.

There are also several more subtle signs that should help you to position yourself in the best place. First, remember that shelter is the top priority of most woodland animals at this time of year: they have to survive some horrendous weather and they stay alive by doing their utmost to avoid the worst of it. Just like you and me, woodpigeons want to sleep in a relatively warm and comfortable place. Unlike us, they don't have

well insulated homes and cosy duvets, but they do like to have the natural equivalent. Investigate areas of woodland that are sheltered by hills and valleys, and then seek out the copses and spinneys that provide the most protection from the elements. When you've narrowed down your search to a particular patch of woodland, investigate the lee side (the side that is most sheltered from prevailing winds) because this is where its inhabitants will find most protection from the weather. Some trees, such as pine species, holly, yew and laurel, keep their leaves through the winter, and pigeons will head for them when they're ready for a snug night's sleep. Similarly, ivy has year-round foliage, which is dense and waxy enough to keep out the rain, so pay close attention to places where the trees are being strangled by thick patches of this evergreen creeper – woodies love to shuffle amongst this stuff for a cosy night's sleep.

When I think I've found an active roost, the next job is to find a hiding place that should enable me to make the most of the opportunity. Pigeons often pitch into the tops of the trees for a good look around before they drop into thicker, more sheltered cover as the light starts to fade, so it pays to be within range of one or two of these early vantage points. As the air rifle hunter is limited to taking static shots, range is an important consideration, and I try to set up within about 30 metres of a stand of two or three trees that I expect incoming birds to flight to.

For the reasons discussed earlier, birds tend to favour roosts in more overgrown areas of woodland so expect your marksmanship to be tested to the full as you do your best to thread your pellet through the twigs to its mark. Try to find a place where such obstacles are minimal because they'll easily knock an airgun pellet off its course. An evening's shooting can be ruined by fine twigs getting in the way: they are hard to spot when the light starts to fade and harder still when they're out of focus in your scope.

I don't usually build a full hide for roost shooting forays because it's handy to be able to

*Wear a headnet to stop your face showing like a beacon in winter woodland.*

one pigeon takes flight the rest of the flock will usually follow, so avoiding detection is essential. I use a simple little trick that takes just a couple of seconds yet makes my movements so much quieter. The woodland floor is usually littered with brittle twigs and crisp, dry leaves that crack and crunch under the lightest of footfalls. This inconvenient source of noise is easily avoided by simply using the side of your foot to shove all the debris away from your shooting place before you settle down for the evening. By clearing a patch in this way, you'll expose the soft, moist, spongy humus beneath the crunchy leaf litter. You can move about silently on this stuff, carefully shifting your weight and adjusting your aim without risk of being heard by edgy woodpigeons.

When hunting pigeons at the roost, I try to get myself into position a couple of hours before sunset. Roosting time can vary slightly from place to place, but the important thing is to try to get there before the pigeons start streaming in. Move quietly into position, load-up and make any final adjustments to clothing and kit. There are frequently times when I leave it too late and turn up just in time to catch the last few arrivals, but sport never seems to be as good after early birds have been spooked from their perches by the clumsy arrival of a flummoxed hunter.

In terms of timing, you'll be onto a real winner if you can swing it so your outing coincides with an evening when local shot-gunners are out targeting pigeons in neighbouring woods. Understandably, the racket of booming shotguns unsettles pigeons and keeps them on the move, so you can expect plenty to get pushed in your direction. The quiet muzzle report of your silenced airgun will be barely audible compared with the din of the shotguns, and the woodies will assume that the woods where you are hiding offer sanctuary from the noisy barrage of lead shot. I've had some cracking evenings sniping woodpigeons that have been displaced by booming 12-bores; the majority of them in tiny patches of woodland to which the birds have fled to avoid the thunderous onslaught of the local pigeon shoot.

move if you set up in the wrong place. My typical choice of cover is the shaded side of a thick tree trunk. Rather than sitting, I usually stand and wait, as this means I'm able to shuffle around the tree depending on where shots present themselves, and can use the trunk as a support to steady my aim. However, I will occasionally throw up a camouflage net to act as a backdrop if there's a shortage of natural cover where I want to position myself – the extra concealment can sometimes help to put a bonus crow, magpie or squirrel in the bag too.

What is really important is to wear full camouflage because pigeons have an awesome ability to spot pink areas of flesh shining through the gloom – and they'll go clattering off as soon as they do. For this reason, I would recommend wearing a headnet and gloves to hide all your telltale pink bits. These inexpensive accessories will also help to keep out the evening chill as the temperature starts to fall.

Keeping quiet is as important as keeping out of sight. Woodpigeons are naturally wary birds and they're easily spooked by unexpected sounds from the undergrowth beneath their roosting trees. Most frustrating for the hunter is the fact that if

Weather conditions can also influence the habits of incoming pigeons. Frankly, I love to be in the woods on still winter's evenings when there's the sort of nip in the air that sends your breath billowing though your headnet in steamy plumes, but these aren't generally the best conditions for hunting. Although it's easier to appreciate the woodland environment in calm weather, pigeons tend to gather in larger flocks when the weather turns rough. Also, because they don't like having to hang on for dear life while being buffeted about in the treetops, woodies usually swoop in lower when there's a stiff breeze blowing. Apart from resulting in closer shots at less challenging angles, the shaking and creaking of branches caused by wind rattling through the trees also helps to mask the unavoidable sounds and movements that can expose the presence of a hunter. The only downside is that you may be presented with a bobbing target.

Wet weather doesn't tend to be associated with fruitful roost shooting. Pigeons are reluctant to fly far when there's rain falling and will often settle down to sleep in trees close to wherever they've been feeding, rather than getting soaked during the journey back to their favourite roost. Likewise, woodies often sit tight when it's foggy. The reduced visibility makes it difficult for them to navigate so they'll stay where they are rather than risk getting lost on the way back to their usual haunts.

When the wind is really blowing, pigeons tend to zip into the woods and straight onto a branch without much deliberation. In this situation, it's usually best to stay quite still until they settle. In my experience, incoming pigeons tend to be very edgy for a few moments after landing: scanning all around for danger until they gradually begin to relax. The more birds there are, the greater the risk of being rumbled and it's an anxious time as dozens of pairs of eyes scrutinise the surrounding area for signs of danger. Eventually, the birds' body language will tell you that they're beginning to settle: they'll slump down into a less upright posture and may even begin to preen themselves or waddle along the branches. This is the time to choose your bird and gingerly raise the rifle.

On a still evening, the arrival of the birds is usually signalled by the faint whistle of wings, and the excitement really peaks when a flock of birds circles overhead in preparation for landing. When pigeons are spiralling down in this way, you've got a little more time to ready yourself for the shot. Wait until they pass over you and lift the gun as

*A combination of full camouflage and shade helps to hide the hunter as woodpigeons circle in to roost.*

they're going away so they can't see the movement. If you miss this opportunity, you'll have another chance to raise your gun as they flap down, with wings paddling backwards to control their rate of descent. At this stage, the pigeons will be looking down at their feet and distracted by the manoeuvres required to make a tidy landing. It's a brief opportunity and if you miss it, you'd be well advised to sit tight and wait until they drop their guard.

With a pigeon in your sights, you're presented with the kill area conundrum. It's a subject that seems to cause much excitement in the letters pages of the airgun press and on the various

*When the woodies have landed, the shooter has to ensure that his shot hits the mark.*

internet forums, where countless 'armchair experts' spout off from behind their keyboards. When it comes to the argument of where to place your pellet, there appear to be many self-proclaimed experts willing to dish out instructions, but I'm afraid there really is no definitive answer other than to opt for precision.

That big pink breast stands out like a beacon in the golden rays of the setting February sun: it's big and inviting but don't be tempted. In my experience, a shot to the front of the chest is one of the worst you can make with a legal limit airgun because the vital organs (namely the heart and lungs) are virtually armour-plated by feather, bones, muscle and a crop full of food. At a slightly more sideward angle, a strike just below the 'elbow' of the wing is far more likely to cause fast and fatal damage to vital organs. Direct hits between the shoulders from behind are effective when shooting 'flat', but they are unlikely to connect with the 'engine room' when you're shooting up at a steep angle. Personally, I try to hit pigeons in the head in most hunting situations. If the shot is a good one, the impact of a solid head shot will literally poleaxe woodpigeons from their perches and they'll be dead before they hit the ground. I've clean missed plenty of them, but I've never known a bird to fly-on after a shot through the skull, and a botched shot that results in a strike to the neck tends to have the same effect. The other outcome is a clean miss, and that does no harm to anything apart from your pride. There's no denying that it takes a reasonable degree of marksmanship to drop pigeons with head shots, but it's a standard that's within the reach of most. Remember also that if you choose the right place and hunt with stealth, you'll probably be shooting at ranges of little more than 20 metres.

And don't forget to lean: the tree trunk that you're hiding behind can also be used to provide support when you take shots. The extra stability of a rested shot vastly improves accuracy, especially if you use a recoilless pre-charged airgun, which you can literally lean directly against whatever kind of rest you are able to exploit. It's a bit different with recoiling spring-powered guns because they should always be shot using the same hold, as they can kick erratically when rested on different surfaces. Nonetheless, you can still lean yourself into the tree trunk, using it to support your hand, arm or shoulder for

*Two plump woodpigeons bagged on a winter's evening.*

hunting roosting pigeons with a sound-moderated air rifle is the fact that the muzzle blast often goes undetected by the birds. There have been plenty of times when I have completely missed a difficult head shot, only for the oblivious bird to stay put so I was able to make the next one count. There have also been numerous occasions when I've dropped a bird from a group and its startled flock mates have taken to the wing, circled once or twice overhead and then dropped straight back into the same tree. For this reason, I would suggest that you hold your position – providing you are satisfied that the bird you shot is cleanly killed and doesn't need to be dispatched – because it's possible that the chance to add another bird to the bag will quickly arise. Remember to carefully mark the place where each pigeon drops so you can easily find it when it's time to make the retrieve. It's surprising just how tricky it can be to find woodies when they're sprawled out on the deck, and it gets a whole lot trickier as darkness falls.

added stability, as long as you keep the gun clear and maintain your usual hold. Taking a leaning shot certainly doesn't amount to cheating: it is merely another means of ensuring precision, and I do it whenever I can.

The rhythmic bobbing caused by wind moving through the branches does add to the difficulty of head shots, although it's just a matter of timing, which can easily be achieved with experience. Of course, timing depends on range and rate of movement but, as a guide, you should be aiming to touch-off the trigger just as the shot is about to line up. Wait until the pigeon's head has reached the centre of the crosshairs and it'll bounce away again before your pellet reaches the mark. Get it right and the satisfaction of sending a woodpigeon crashing into the leaves takes some beating.

One of the most wonderful things about

## The attraction of ivy

One of the biggest draws to virtually all animals in the winter time is food. Wild creatures have to spend virtually every hour of daylight foraging for nourishment because pickings are scarce; find the places that offer the easiest sources of nutrition and you'll find quarry species trying to exploit them.

Pigeons are a major agricultural pest: the damage they do to crops, and the consequent cost they cause to farmers, is well documented, but even this food source can be unreliable in the winter. When the weather turns really cold, ground

*Ivy berries can attract pigeons in numbers when food is thin on the ground.*

crops can often be frozen solid and rendered unmanageable for the pigeon's beak, or simply hidden beneath an impenetrable covering of snow. It's at these times that the hunter has to look above the ground; ivy berries are what you want.

Hard, black ivy berries are poisonous to humans and are presumably not very appealing to woodpigeons because they don't tend to feed on them when there are other choices on their menu. But when times get really tough, bunches of these shiny berries provide a vital source of nutrition and the woodies know it. Furthermore, the dense, waxy leaves of this parasitic climber also lend cover from wind, rain and snow. So ivy provides food with the added bonus of shelter: two of the fundamental elements required for survival.

Woodies tend to target the ivy clumps with the heaviest fruit, and they don't seem to mind if the ivy berries are frozen solid. They presumably swallow down the berries the same as they would eat any hard fruit or seed and then let them defrost in their crop.

When the pigeons find a rich supply of ivy berries, most often on the outer edges of the woods where they're easy to spot, they tend to keep coming back until they've exhausted the supply. Although you're not likely to encounter huge flocks of birds feeding in this way, it's not unusual to come across as many as a dozen or so birds feeding on the same patch. They get into all

sorts of contortions, sometimes hanging upside down as they clamber precariously on the dangling vines. From time to time they'll flap violently in an effort to keep a balance on their precarious footing while plucking the berries off with their beaks. It's a telltale sound you'll sometimes hear as you creep quietly through winter woods: it's the hunter's cue to ready himself for a shot.

Stalking feeding pigeons takes a lot of stealth, and the first challenge lies in locating exactly where the birds are so you can choose the best route to avoid detection. When I hear that characteristic fluttering of wings, I freeze dead still and listen very carefully. If you can hear the woodies, the chances are that they're pretty close – maybe even within range. If they're close enough for a shot, you'll need to raise the gun oh so slowly to avoid detection. Often, you'll need to creep a little closer to get yourself within range, and it's a lot easier if you can spot where the birds are. If you can see them, or at least some of them, try to gingerly shift position to get some cover between yourself and your quarry. It might be a thick tree trunk, a spindly bush or even another dense patch of ivy. If you can, get yourself behind this obstruction and use it as a screen as you advance slowly and as quietly as you can.

More frequently, this is a hunting opportunity that lends itself best to an ambush. If you've managed to earmark an abundant patch of ivy that's receiving regular visits, it can be beneficial to set up a discreet hide, perhaps based around a camouflage net or just a few fallen branches carefully arranged to keep you hidden. Decoys can also add to the appeal, suggesting to passing pigeons that there's a food source here and others are confidently tucking in with abandon. Again, this tactic works best on the outer edge of the woods where the decoys can easily be seen. It pays to get them right up among the ivy – a task made easier by lofting poles if you have a set. And don't be afraid to use one or two deeks with wide open wings because they'll create the effect of the flapping birds struggling to keep a purchase on the dangling ivy.

*Lurk amongst dense patches of ivy when the weather is cold and you can expect to encounter pigeons.*

More often than not, you can expect to happen across opportunities of pigeons on ivy when you're just mooching around the woods without the luxury of a hide or decoys. It is for reasons like this that I always keep a headnet and gloves stowed in a pocket of my hunting jacket. They cover what would otherwise be the pink blobs of my head and hands, and enable me to set up an impromptu ambush around suitable natural cover. Whether hiding behind a tree trunk, lurking among the gloomy shadows of light-blocking yew-trees, or sitting against a pile of logs left by the foresters, you should get shots at pigeons drawn in by the lure of the ivy berries by covering up and keeping still.

Ivy berries are very dry and bitter, and pigeon meat can become subtly infused with the flavour when they're feeding exclusively on this late winter fruit. Don't be discouraged from eating them, though. It's a very mild flavour at most, and virtually undetectable, so these birds are still as good as ever for the table.

# Shelter on the farm

The perennial appeal of the farmyard doesn't wane at all in the winter. Quarry species were drawn here by the promise of nesting sites in the spring and to seek shelter from the burning sun during the height of summer. Now it is much-needed protection from the cold, combined with a ready supply of food, that's pulling pests into the farm buildings.

In the hands of a safe and responsible shooter, the quiet and precise air rifle is the perfect tool for controlling pests around the farm. It's no secret that legal limit (sub-12ft.lb) airguns are relatively low in the power stakes. Although this can sometimes be perceived as a disadvantage, when it comes to controlling vermin around farmyards, the limited power of the air rifle is actually a huge advantage.

Shooting around the confines of agricultural buildings presents the shooter with a long list of

*The shelter of a farm building can save a shooting session when the weather turns foul.*

*When avian pests target the farmyard, they often land in adjacent trees before swooping down to feed.*

potential hazards that must be considered and overcome before you even think about pulling the trigger. A gun with too much grunt just wouldn't be safe to use in such a situation, but with a little forethought, and the safe use of backstops, nothing beats an airgun when it comes to close-quarters farmyard vermin control. As previously explained in the passages on hunting around farmyards in the 'Spring' and 'Summer' sections of this book, the presence of workers and livestock means safe shooting is paramount. So always make sure you're aware of any hazards before embarking on a farmyard foray.

Quarry species including collard doves, feral pigeons, jackdaws and even crows, magpies and the occasional woodpigeon can be encountered around the farmyard at this time of year, and often at relatively close quarters. Farm units provide birds with shelter from biting winds and icy cold rain and snow. Even out in the yard, the windbreak created by the buildings provides avian quarry with far more protection than they'd find out in the open countryside.

Apart from keeping birds warm and dry, the farmyard also provides them with a seemingly endless supply of food. It's no surprise that the worst pest infestations on dairy farms occur when the herd is brought inside for the winter months. Scavenging doves and jackdaws quickly home in on the drifts of nutritious silage put out as forage feed for barn-bound cattle. I should also imagine the heat emitted by a hundred or so steaming, huffing cows raises the temperature inside the unit by a degree or two, thus adding to its appeal on a bitterly cold winter's day. Cattle also need to drink considerable volumes of water to produce all those litres of milk. Indoor water troughs can bring avian pests flocking when outdoor water sources are frozen solid.

Most pleasing of all is the fact that farmyards offer the same degree of shelter and comfort to the shooter as they do his quarry. The protection they provide from the elements can often rescue a shooting session on a day when the cutting cold wind or relentless rain makes woodland hunting a rather uninviting prospect. I'm always grateful to be able to retreat to the farm on occasions when foul weather would otherwise force me to abandon my outing altogether.

There's nothing worse than being rained off after you've spent a long, hard week at work looking forward to your weekend shooting session, but the farmyard is one place where the air rifle hunter can count on finding some shelter from the elements when gales and squally showers make exposed places somewhat less appealing than usual. Although slopping around a filthy farmyard isn't quite as exhilarating as roost shooting in remote woodlands, it's a sight more fun that sitting at home watching rain running down the window. Also, you're providing a useful service: I've secured some of my best shooting permissions by first winning the landowner's trust by thinning out feral pigeons, crows or magpies around farm units. Now that I'm allowed to wander their pheasant coverts in pursuit of woodpigeons for the pot, my hosts still expect me to keep the farmyard free from uninvited guests. So, by spending the occasional rainy afternoon

*Hay bales provide the ultimate in warmth and comfort when targeting pests on the farmyard.*

skulking around the barns when the weather is too grim to do much else, I'm also helping to keep my side of the deal. And, even if action is a little thin on the ground, at least I can find a warm, dry place to sit down and enjoy a flask of tea while dodging the domestic chores!

I find the best way to approach these sessions is to locate whatever it is that's attracting pests – a feed store, stock pens or whatever – and then try to find a place from which to ambush the birds as they home in. Rather than trying to target your quarry inside of buildings, it's often easier, and safer, to ambush them as they approach. More often than not, birds will land on a rooftop, grain silo or in the uppermost branches of some adjacent tree, so they can scan for danger before they swoop down to feed. Providing there's a safe backdrop, these can be excellent places to pick off your quarry; you can even use one or two decoys to lure them in.

A pair of magpie or pigeon deeks set out in the yard with a few fistfuls of animal feed or grain to give the impression of a feeding scenario can work wonders when hungry birds are surveying the farmyard. The ruse of using crow decoys and chunks of bread can also work well: suggesting that corvids are plundering the leftovers from a farm worker's lunch. Keep an eye on the ground too because, although rats are mostly nocturnal in their habits, you could well see the odd one or two scuttling about during daylight hours. And even if you don't actually see any rats, you may find signs – such as holes, footprints and droppings – that indicate a place worth visiting with your lamping gear after nightfall.

Even when targeting pest birds when they're outside of the buildings, there's no reason why you can't take advantage of the cover and shelter on the inside. Hides frequently come ready-made around farm units, so you'll often be able to hide yourself in the shady gloom of an outbuilding, amongst the machinery or behind stacks of pallets. Search around and you should be able to find a secluded place where you can make yourself comfortable and take supported shots.

As far as I'm concerned, the haystack and straw bales represent the pinnacle of luxury when it comes to farmyard shooting in the winter and, by shifting a few bales, you should be able to create a very warm, stable and comfy shooting station that provides good cover and steady shots. Just remember to check with the farmer before you go tampering with stacked bales, and exercise caution because they're deceptively heavy and prone to collapse when piled high. Remember also to return anything you move back to the place where you found it when you're finished.

# Lamping rats

Rats swarm to farmyards in the winter, and shooting these pests by lamplight provides some of the most hectic action the airgun shooter could hope to encounter. It can also be surprisingly comfortable: shooting within the shelter of a farm building on nights when the weather is far too harsh for lamping rabbits out on the hills. Not only does ratting offer busy sport on cold winter's nights, it also provides a service that will be welcomed by many farmers who go to great lengths, and expense, to reduce numbers of these notorious pests.

Most farms have a resident population of rats throughout the year, which doesn't cause too much of a problem until after the autumn, when a lack of natural cover and food sends legions of ravenous rodents marching in from the fields, hedges, riverbanks and woods. The appeal of the farmyard to overwintering rats can be attributed to several factors: farm buildings provide protection from the elements during the toughest time of the year; older farms in particular are usually riddled with nooks and crannies where these adaptable rodents can hide and nest. What's more, farms offer a plentiful and easily accessible supply of food at a time when nature's larder is all but empty.

The arrival of the winter influx of brown rats is bad news for the farmer. Hundreds of hungry

*When the cattle are moved inside for winter, rats are quickly attracted by the filth.*

– so never touch rats with your bare hands and be very careful anywhere you think these rodents may be present. The disease can survive for a considerable time outside of rats' bodies as long as it's in a moist environment – after they have urinated in ditches, puddles, ponds and animal troughs, for example – so the shooter must be ever-vigilant. Never be tempted to tuck into a packed lunch around places frequented by rats and always wash your hands thoroughly after a ratting session. I carry a bottle of alcohol-based antiseptic hand-wash with my rat shooting kit so I can clean my hands immediately and thus eliminate the threat of cross-infection.

Weil's disease, which you'll also hear referred to as leptospirosis, is incredibly dangerous if not treated promptly. Symptoms to look out for include aches and pains, fever, chills, loss of appetite and nausea. The early stages of Weil's disease are easily mistaken for a dose of common flu, but it becomes far more aggressive in its later stages and advanced symptoms range from bruising of the skin, sore eyes and anaemia, to nose bleeds and jaundice. Symptoms usually appear within a few days of infection but can take several weeks to manifest so must always be borne in mind by the rat shooter. In most cases, and given prompt diagnosis, victims make a full recovery following treatment with antibiotics, but the illness can result in permanent damage to internal organs and can even cause death.

Should you ever feel feverish or experience flu-like symptoms after shooting in a place that holds rats, get yourself checked over by a doctor. It's important to make them aware of the possibility of Weil's disease because it's a condition that many GPs are unfamiliar with.

If I haven't put you off completely (and I hope I haven't because the disease threat is easily

rodent mouths feeding on grain stores and animal feed soon eat into their profits, but the biggest threat comes from the numerous unpleasant diseases carried by these uninvited guests. Rats urinate and defecate all around their territories, even where they eat. And, bearing in mind that some of the lurgies you can pick up from their excrement can be fatal, rats are the last pest anyone would want in places where food is reared, produced or stored for human consumption.

This threat of disease has to be at the forefront of the shooter's mind whenever targeting rats. Rats are famous, or more accurately infamous, for being the carrier of bubonic plague, the Black Death, which caused an enormous death toll across Europe and Asia during the 14th and 18th centuries. Although the plague was spread by the black rat (an animal that's now incredibly scarce in the UK), its bigger cousin, the brown rat, carries countless nasty diseases and its population has spiralled at an alarming rate since it first arrived in Britain in the early 18th century.

Despite gaining notoriety through the Black Death, the biggest threat that rats pose to shooters is Weil's disease. This infection is spread through bites and contact with blood, urine and droppings overcome if you take sensible precautions) you'll want to know where to go looking for the cream of the winter ratting action. Pig and poultry farms are real favourites with these scavenging rodents because they tend to offer an abundance of nutritious animal feed around holding pens, as well as lots of places for Ratty to hide. I also think rats home in quickly on such holdings because they stink so much: they must be able to literally smell them from miles away. Dairy farms also appeal to rats because they too provide food and shelter, usually in the shape of maize silage and animal bedding when the herd is brought inside during the colder months. You'll also find rats lurking around grain stores and places where food crops and animal feed are stored. Some of my best rat shooting is on a farm that has no livestock at all. In fact, it's a market garden that produces vegetables for some of the country's finest restaurants. When the temperature starts to fall at the end of the autumn, rats move into the huge, festering compost heaps. These steaming piles of reject vegetables are composted down to create a rich soil improver that nourishes future crops, but the process of decomposition generates warmth, which keeps rats toasty during even the coldest weather. By setting up home in these heaps during the winter months, rats get to enjoy fine dining on organic vegetables in the comfort of a centrally-heated nest.

Generally speaking, the farms that suffer worst with rats tend to be located on or close to watercourses. These nomadic rodents use streams, ditches and rivers like highways and, as soon as the farmer has managed to fend off one infestation with an expensive poisoning regime, you can bet that another influx is just around the corner. The old-fashioned, tumbledown farms are also more vulnerable than modern holdings. The simple fact is that rustic farmsteads made of stone and wood have more of the gaps, cracks and general clutter where rats can hide and multiply than state-of-the-art concrete fortresses.

Once you've secured yourself some rat shooting, you'll need the right kit to tackle them.

I favour a .22 calibre airgun for ratting because, although they're not exactly massive, these hardy rodents are tough little critters. They may be at the top of the vermin list but they still deserve to be treated with the same respect as all other quarry species, and that means you have a duty to ensure that they come to a swift end. I almost always take head shots when ratting, and it's not as tricky as it sounds as this sort of shooting is usually conducted at ranges of between 10 and 20 metres. The extra clout provided by a heavy .22 pellet helps to stop rats dead in their tracks, whereas a .177 often whizzes right through with less of an impact. Although the ultimate result of a head shot with either calibre is immediate death, rats that have been 'drilled' by a .177 pellet are inclined to run on a few feet before they keel over, which can make them tricky to retrieve at the end of the session. The wallop of a .22 generally sprawls them out immediately, as does the mighty .25 if you favour the giant calibre. Some shooters like to use hollow-point ammunition for even more clout when shooting rats, but I prefer to stick with the same high quality domed pellets I use for all my shooting. Familiarity means that I know how these pellets perform, I know they are accurate and I know that a rat is not going to get up again if I plant one between its eye and ear.

If you're choosing a gun especially for rat shooting, go for something compact because

*A hungry rat makes a raid on the chicken run as the light begins to fade.*

*A gun-mounted lamp is a vital weapon in the rat shooter's arsenal, providing light wherever the gun is pointed.*

you're likely to be using it in the confines of farm buildings. Longer barrels tend to get knocked and scratched when used in sheds and barns after dark. It's also very useful to have a multi-shot, magazine-fed gun for lamping. Ratting action can be fast and furious and you'll be able to fully exploit opportunities as they're presented if you can quickly reload with the throw of a bolt or sidelever rather than having to rummage in your pocket for a pellet and then try to fumble it into the breech in complete darkness.

One very important, and very obvious, piece of kit you're going to need for lamping rats is a lamp. There are loads of suitable models on the market but some are better than others. First and foremost, you want a gun-mounted lamp: the type that clips onto your scope and provides illumination to light up the sight picture wherever you point your air rifle. Unless you also intend to

use the lamp for rabbiting, there's no need to go for a particularly powerful model because you'll only be using it over relatively short distances. If you do opt for a very bright lamp, make sure it has variable power so you can wind it down for

*Coloured filters help to soften lamplight when rats are skittish.*

close-range ratting, otherwise you'll spook the rats and they'll refuse to come out. The best lamps also provide the option of adding coloured filters. While I'm not convinced about the manufacturers' claims about quarry species being less able to see coloured light, I do appreciate being able to soften the beam with a red or amber filter if the rats are being 'lamp shy'. One thing I am particularly fussy about is how easy a lamp is to clip on and off the scope tube. Some great lamps have terrible mounting systems with fiddly screw-mount attachments that take ages to fix on and remove. This isn't really a problem if your intention is to set up your gun as a dedicated ratting tool, but it's a right pain in the backside if you want to be able to quickly take it on and off to switch between day and night hunting requirements. My favourite lamp mounts are the ones that clip on and off with a well-designed catch that doesn't require any tools.

Another handy piece of kit I always take ratting is a backpack stool. The integral, fold-out seat means I've always got a firm, comfortable and clean place to sit as well as being able to carry useful accessories. These little extras include a torch, a tough pair of gloves and tongs or pliers for clearing away shot rats, and whatever holding bait I decide to use to keep the rats still while I take my shots – more on that in a moment.

Once you're equipped for the job, it's a wise move to visit the farm for a daytime recce so you can get the measure of the place before it gets dark. This observational visit should enable you to identify hot spots to target when the rats start venturing out at dusk. As well as looking for signs of rats, safety should also be at the forefront of your mind: farms are potentially dangerous places at the best of times and even more so when it's pitch black. Identify a spot where you'll be able to shoot safely, preferably against a solid backstop of concrete that will eliminate any risk to you, farm workers, buildings, machinery or livestock. Also look out for any other hazards you may encounter and plan a safe route around the farmyard thus avoiding any dangerous obstacles.

With regard to finding evidence of rats, there are plenty of signs to look out for. Their distinctive holes are usually easy to find around banks, among heaps of rubble, compost or other waste, and along the edges of buildings and fences. These burrows are usually quite exposed as busy footfall results in areas of smooth, barren soil around the entrance. Ratty traffic also causes the classic rat-runs (clearly defined little tracks across dirt or through grass and other vegetation) that connect the holes where the rodents live with the places they visit to forage food. If the ground is soft and muddy, you'll even find the footprints of the rats that travel along these routes. As a rough rule of thumb, you can assume the busiest areas are those with the most footprints or where the runs are particularly smooth and worn. Another classic rat calling card is their excrement: dark, cigar-shaped pellets of about two centimetres in length that you're unlikely to confuse with anything else. As with rabbit droppings, you can get a rough idea of how long they've been hanging around as they're darker and shinier when fresh and become dry and faded after exposure to the elements. Find a scattering of moist, black 'slugs' and you can assume that they were left behind during a very recent visit by a rat. Finally, you can sometimes identify the presence of rats by their gnawing. Feed sacks that are leaking their contents through nibbled holes with frayed edges have probably been nibbled by rats. You may even come across chewed vegetables that have been got at by these hungry rodents and, in extreme cases, they've even been known to munch through plaster and chomp through electrical wires.

Once I've got a rough idea of the areas that are being visited by rats, I turn my attention to keeping the fidgety rodents still for long enough for me to compose that all-important head shot. This is best achieved by offering some kind of feed to persuade scuttling rats to stop and eat. In the early days of my hunting apprenticeship, I started out by offering samples of whatever they were feeding on at the farm (everything from cow cake and pig nuts to grain and rotten vegetables) and, although the rats accepted my offerings, I was often left frustrated after they grabbed a mouthful and ran off before I'd had time to take aim. So I went back to the drawing board.

Finding the ultimate bait that is smelly enough to attract these scavenging rodents and of the right consistency to keep them still, while also being relatively clean to handle is a tall order. I've still yet to find the perfect solution but I have managed to narrow my choice down to a few firm favourites.

In my opinion, nothing beats liquidised cat food in terms of sheer attraction. It has served me well since I first struck upon the idea well over a decade ago and, if you opt for a really fishy flavour, a dollop of this sloppy gloop will stop any passing rat in its tracks. Furthermore, because it's been liquidised in a food processor, rats can't just grab chunks and run off: they have stop and lap it up, and that provides the shooter with crucial time to aim.

Unfortunately, liquidised cat food has its downfalls. The stench that gives this stuff its appeal to rats also makes the wreaking goo an absolute nightmare to handle. Once blitzed into a soup, the resulting oily sludge leaks from just about any vessel and sticks to everything it comes into contact with, and it has a smell that really lingers – even if you wear gloves, the odour seems to permeate. Making it is quite a hassle too, and it takes a very tolerant partner to let you process batches of liquidised cat food in the family kitchen and then store it in the freezer until it's required.

In a bid to find a more user-friendly holding bait for rats, I've tried a few alternatives over the years. For convenience and ease of handling, peanut butter and chocolate spread take some beating. They're easy to obtain and come packed in a jar ready to go and, unlike the offensive whiff of cat food, these sweet treats actually smell very nice. Nobody's going to complain if you come home smelling of chocolate are they?

In my experience, peanut butter and chocolate spread don't appeal to Ratty quite as much as the fishy cat food sludge, and the former is probably the more productive of the two. Nonetheless, rats will usually stop for a sniff and a lick if you use a

*This hole is a sure sign of rats, and is a good place to lay some bait.*

spoon to smear either of these 'clean' baits on a wall or on the ground along their favourite runs.

During recent sessions, I've been trialling another supermarket bait with considerable success. Marmite is a bit stickier and messier than the sweet spreads, but it has a strong savoury whiff and its consistency means that rats have to stop and lap it up if they want a decent feed. Rather than just spooning out Marmite along runs, I've been putting dollops onto large, flat pebbles collected from the beach. These portable 'trays' of holding bait can easily be picked up and moved to another spot, but are heavy enough not to get blown around on a breezy evening.

Another recent addition to my menu of holding baits is fishing pellets. These nutritious little morsels of fishmeal are used by anglers to attract fish. In very small sizes, they hold fish in the pre-baited area by keeping them grubbing around, and they appear to have a similar effect on rats. You can get them in sizes from two millimetres to more than 20 millimetres in diameter, but you'll need the really small ones to keep rats still; offer them the big ones and they'll just grab them and run away to devour them in some hidden lair. Fishing pellets come in a variety of flavours too, but the fishiest ones seem to have the greatest appeal. The best thing about these offerings is the fact that they are dry and relatively cheap. You can bag them up and handle them without any fuss or mess. Being inexpensive, they can easily be bought in bulk and even stored in your boot, then used to pre-bait a spot you intend to target. They don't always have the immediate appeal of the gooey baits mentioned above, but if you feed them for a few evenings prior to the hunt, the rats should be foraging with confidence when you turn up with your airgun.

When I arrive for the cull, I'll be aiming to get on site a good hour before sunset. After spending a long winter's day holed-up, rats usually head out foraging with a flurry of activity at dusk, so I like to make sure I'm ready and waiting in time for this highly productive period.

This is when the earlier investigations pay off because I'll be hoping to set up an ambush somewhere between the burrows where the rats have been nesting during the day and the food source they'll be creeping out to raid come nightfall. Bearing in mind that rats tend to stick to the same runs, which usually follow edges such as the walls of buildings, try to set baits along these ratty corridors because that's where they are most likely to be noticed by your quarry. Of course, it is essential that you are able to easily see the baits when they're set out because that's where you'll be taking your shots later on; ensure also that the bait spots are located in places where your shots will be safe. If you've got a companion with you, get yourself into position and then send them out to set the baits so you can direct them to exactly the right spot. The last thing you want to find is that you've got a really productive bait spot attracting a steady trickle of rats, but you're unable to get a clear shot because there's an obstruction like a clump of grass or piece of machinery in the way. More often than not, I position myself wherever I expect to get maximum action, even if it's outside. However, if it's raining or particularly cold, I'll settle for what might be a less productive area so I can take advantage of a more sheltered position inside a farm building.

With the baits set, it's just a matter of sitting back and awaiting a response. Rats are boisterous creatures so don't be surprised to hear them bickering before you spot them. The squeaking and scratching of scrapping rats under pallets, among the straw bales or in some dark corner of

*The variety of sizes in this winter haul proves the rat's ability to breed throughout the year.*

the barn, are all part and parcel of the rat shooting experience. Quite often, you'll spot rats on your baits before it gets properly dark. Don't wait on ceremony, leave the lamp off and shoot as you would in normal light to make the most of these early opportunities.

As the light fades, the activity usually peaks as more and more rats venture out in search of food. First, you'll just have to use your lamp to illuminate some of the gloomier corners, but you'll need it to see anything at all before very long. What I do is sit with the lamp off to give the rats confidence to venture out. Then, every so often, I'll shoulder the rifle and flick the lamp on so I can scan each of my bait spots and any other promising areas. While searching out rats in this way, make your sweeps with the lamp slow and steady because erratic movement will cause a sudden shifting of the shadows that can really spook rats; softening the light with a coloured filter can also help to reduce this problem.

When you do spot a rat, you'll probably first notice it from the light reflecting back from its eyes – if you're using a red filter, expect to see beady little eyes burning back at you with a devilish glow. With your scope wound down to five or six-times magnification to let more light in, you should quickly be able to make out the complete form of the rat as you peer through the lens. Line up the crosshairs between its eye and ear, and touch off the shot.

If you shoot a rat and it's cleanly killed, don't be in a rush to retrieve it. The sight of dead rats will not discourage other members of the colony, and I've often shot more as they sit lapping blood from their fallen brethren. Rats can be accused of many things, but wastefulness is not one of them. In fact, on one particular vegetable farm where I shoot, the protein-starved rats can't wait to devour their shot companions and are often spotted, and frequently shot, while they try to drag their mates' corpses back to some hidden place to be devoured.

From time to time, you'll encounter finicky rats that bolt from the lamplight and refuse to venture

*Rats should be cleared away when the shooting is over, but never with your bare hands.*

back out. Keep watching and you'll often notice that the rat hasn't gone to ground but is hiding somewhere close, maybe amongst some rubble or behind the corner of the wall just a few inches from the bait. If these rats have had a taste of whatever bait you put out, it's likely that they'll want to come back for more. Keep the lamp on and stay on aim, because they'll only spook again if you switch it back off and on or start moving it around. Keep looking through the scope and you'll probably be able to see the nervous rat peeping out and then backing in again. Hold steady and there's every chance it will soon become less suspicious of the light and wander back out into full view.

It's often the case that activity tails off or even ceases completely after a couple of productive hours. This can be attributed to reasons including the reduction you've hopefully made in their numbers, the fact that the remaining rats are suspicious of the light and sound that led to the demise of their mates, and because the rats have got to where they want to be and will be staying there until disturbed. There's very little you can do about the sudden decline in ratty activity, and I generally take it as my cue to tidy up and trundle home.

The obvious health hazard posed by rats means their corpses should be disposed of carefully. As previously mentioned, I always carry a stout pair of gloves and a pair of pliers or tongs so I can avoid direct contact. These tools are a last resort, though, and I always have a look around the farm in the hope of finding a shovel or spade that will enable me to carry the bodies from an even safer distance. Find out where the farmer would prefer you to dispose of dead rats – they usually direct me to the fire site – and do your best to safely gather all the retrievable bodies and dump them there when you finish. With the clear-up complete, all that remains is to wash your hands and head home for a good night's sleep.

# Night vision for extreme stealth

The methods I describe for rat shooting can be even more effective when using night vision (NV) optics.

Instead of using normal lamplight, NV sights intensify ambient light from the stars, the moon and other distant sources of illumination to create a monochrome image of silvery green and black. In situations of complete darkness, when ambient light is blocked out by cloud cover or when you are shooting inside buildings, an infra-red booster lamp provides additional 'invisible' light to enhance the image. This lack of illumination in the conventional sense means there's no bright glow to blow your cover like when you're using a normal lamp. The hunter using NV optics is, therefore, totally hidden in a veil of darkness.

Despite their massive technological advantages, NV optics also have their downfalls and I have to say that I still favour a traditional lamp for most of my after-dark hunting. NV equipment is expensive and quite cumbersome, though prices are gradually coming down and units are becoming more compact. Another problem with these optics is that they produce a very flat, one-dimensional sight picture, which makes it difficult to estimate range. This problem is easily rectified by establishing set range markers, either in the form of fixed features in the places where you are shooting – walls, fence posts, trees and suchlike – or markers that you set out yourself.

If you splash out on a dedicated NV scope, you'll have to splash out on a dedicated NV rifle too, otherwise you'll be forever changing optics and constantly re-zeroing as you switch between daytime and night-time hunting assignments. If you're in the position to make such an investment, this hardware will enable you to watch and shoot your quarry as it ventures out in complete darkness, completely oblivious to your presence. One word of warning: flicking on a normal lamp and waving it is usually all it takes to frighten off any rats that get too close for comfort. You don't have that luxury with NV so be prepared for unwanted close encounters and make sure your trousers are tucked into your boots!

For those on a tighter budget, it's possible to purchase NV units that attach to your daytime scope. These were initially available in the form of bulky, front-mounted units, which were very heavy and did nothing for the balance and handling of the gun. More recently, rear-mounted NV attachments that fix over the ocular lens of the scope are becoming more popular and are generally smaller, lighter and much better balanced. Gun-fit is still compromised because the additional length of the optic tends to push the shooter's head a little too far back along the cheek-piece of the stock. Nonetheless, these units give adequate performance for static hunting applications.

A very impressive, and surprisingly affordable recent development in NV technology is the

NiteSite, which enables you to enjoy the performance of your usual daytime scope along with the stealth of night vision.

The system works by fitting an infrared camera onto your scope's eyepiece, which then relays the sight picture to a monitor mounted on top of the scope. The image on the monitor, which includes your scope's crosshairs, then acts as your sighting device. The head-up shooting position required to view the monitor does affect marksmanship, and I find that without the usual contact with the cheek-piece, standing shots are tricky.

This unit really excels when used from a rested position, and is perfect for static ratting when you can sit and use crates, pallets, sacks or straw bales to support the gun. I've also had good results using it to extend my hunting time while spending evenings ambushing rabbits during the warmer months. I simply sprawl out in the field using the static hunting techniques described in the 'Summer' section of this book, and then clip on the NiteSite so I can continue to pick off rabbits after the sun has gone down.

By and large, the vast majority of the shooting I do with NV optics is done from a static position. Stalking is virtually impossible with this kit because you still need a proper torch to see where you're going and that would completely defeat the object of using NV in the first place. Incidentally, it's always important to carry a torch with you on any hunting trip when using NV. These optics don't produce sufficient illumination to light your way, so you'll need a proper light source to move safely to and from your shooting position and for retrieving shot quarry.

*Electronic add-ons enable the modern hunter to see in the dark with his daytime scope.*

# Let it snow

Most would agree that the British countryside is at its most beautiful when gilded in a blanket of fresh snow – it can also be at its most treacherous. Nonetheless, my urge to get out with the gun is greater than ever when faced with some extreme winter weather. By wrapping up warm and keeping a few simple guidelines in mind, you should be able to enjoy some cracking sport in breathtaking surroundings at a time when the less adventurous, fair weather shooters are cooped up in the house.

Most of the previously mentioned methods for targeting quarry around reliable winter feeding stations will be made even more effective after snowfall or during periods of extreme cold. A covering of snow or freezing temperatures will have reduced and concentrated feeding opportunities, so you're even more likely to encounter pests in places where food is still accessible. Sub-zero temperatures will also have raised the hunger levels of quarry species by a bar or two, so they'll be bolder still when they make their raids.

Drink is as important as food for wild animals trying to survive in bitterly cold weather. Although reserves of water are usually plentiful during the winter, they can be locked away for days and even weeks on end when the mercury plunges below zero. During these periods, supplies of accessible water can become quarry hot spots. Running water in ditches and streams, and ponds and pools that have remained unfrozen where sheltered woodland keeps the ambient temperature a degree or two warmer, can be worth investigating because they're likely to receive visits from all sorts of wildlife.

You can also take advantage of the concealment provided by falling snow. I have on several occasions enjoyed great sport at the pigeon roost, sniping birds that were far less wary than usual as the flakes came swirling down. It could be that the birds are reluctant to leave their perches during snowfall (that's certainly the case during heavier blizzards), although it seems to me that their vision is hampered by the flurry of cascading snowflakes, so the hunter is not so likely to be spotted as he lurks beneath. This tactic works best during light snowfall because birds will just sit tight and stop flighting in during heavy flurries. The reluctance to fly during a total white-out concurs with my theory about restricted vision: the birds presumably stay put because they can't navigate. However, if the snowfall seems too heavy for the pigeons to fly to the roost, I would suggest that it's too heavy to venture out – or time to head for home if you're already out. You don't want to get stranded in the woods, the drive home rendered impassable after a heavy blizzard, just because you thought it would be nice to bag a few woodies in the winter wonderland. Let common sense be your guide when distinguishing between braving the elements and being reckless.

It should go without saying that it's vitally important to ensure that you don't succumb to the extreme cold that's making life tricky for your quarry. At a superficial level, feeling cold is a pain in the backside (or more often a pain in the fingers and toes). You can't shoot effectively when you're uncomfortable and shivering, and you can't shoot at all after you've decided enough is enough and given in to the temptation of a warm house and a hot dinner. At the other end of the scale, extreme cold can kill you – and more easily than you might imagine. I once found myself experiencing the early stages of hypothermia and it wasn't funny. I knew I was getting cold, but didn't realise I was getting quite that cold. Then, before I knew what was going on, my vision started closing in, I felt drowsy, couldn't think straight and could barely put one foot in front of the other. Fortunately, I had a friend with me who helped me back to the car. Things could have turned out very differently if I'd been on my own.

My advice to anyone is to call it a day as soon as you start to feel shivery or uncomfortable in the cold. If you notice strange things happening to your vision or start feeling confused or clumsy,

*Dress accordingly and you'll still be able to enjoy your shooting when the temperature drops below zero.*

take action very quickly because one of the most lethal symptoms of hypothermia is the inability to make good decisions. If you're with a mate, let them know you're feeling unwell so they can help you – it's not being a wimp, it's being sensible. If you're on your own, phone somebody and let them know exactly where you are and then quickly get back to your car, the farmhouse or wherever you can get some warmth. If you decide to warm up in your car, don't attempt to drive home until you're convinced that you've fully recovered because you'll not be safe behind the wheel as long as your judgement is impaired by the cold.

Fortunately, reasonable preparation is usually all it takes to keep the cold at bay and that should start at home. I like to begin a winter field day with a hearty breakfast – running on empty in harsh weather is asking for trouble. My choice is usually a fry-up, but you just need something that will give you a good, slow release of energy, so porridge or a decent helping of toast will suffice if you don't fancy the greasy option. That's the kick-start taken care of, now you need to think about what you'll need when you're out there. If it's really cold, I'll always take a flask of hot tea, coffee or even soup with me – mostly because it's a nice treat to sit down and enjoy a steaming hot drink, but also because it could be a life-saver. Should you find yourself forced into a retreat because the cold is getting the better of you, getting something hot in your belly will help to speed-up your recovery. Incidentally, I can't advocate taking a nip of something a bit stronger to stave off the winter chill. While I enjoy a drink or six as much as anyone, booze and guns don't mix. Furthermore, seemingly warming drinks like brandy only give the impression of creating warmth. This false impression, along with the tendency to further compromise your judgement, could land you in real danger if things start to get dicey. What I do always keep in my bag, though, are a couple of cereal bars. These light snacks may not be as exciting as the contents of a hip flask but they're a damned sight more useful when hunger starts to set in. For longer sessions, I'll also take a round or two of sandwiches, and perhaps a bar of chocolate or a slab of cake to help keep my energy levels up.

The logical way to keep warm during freezing conditions is to stay on the move. A roving session, trudging across snow-covered fields or crunching through brittle, frost-hardened leaves will get your metabolism into full swing, generating plenty of heat as you burn through the calories. Such outings can be really enjoyable: taking in the scenery and observing the tracks left behind by all the wild creatures when there's a covering of snow. Unfortunately, they're not usually the most productive days for the simple fact that it's difficult to crunch across a frozen landscape with any degree of stealth. The most effective approach is usually to set up an ambush at one of those feeding stations, and you'll certainly need to be dressed appropriately if you're going to sit it out for any length of time.

Whether hunting on the move or static, it makes sense to wear plenty of layers. My standard outfit includes a vest, long-sleeved shirt, woolly jumper and fleece, over which I'll wear my usual weatherproof hunting jacket. A lot of people tend to overlook what they wear on their legs but I would certainly recommend investing in a pair of lined, or even better quilted, trousers with a shell of one of the silent, waterproof, modern camouflage materials if you're going to be doing any amount of cold weather shooting. They'll make life a lot more comfortable.

Your choice of footwear will then be dictated by the conditions you're presented with. I have a pair of thermal moonboots that are used by cold storage workers and guaranteed to keep your toes toasty in temperatures down to -40°C. The trouble is, although they're super-warm, they don't offer much flexibility of movement and their treads provide barely any grip, so while they're great for sessions when I'm sat waiting for rats, they're useless for stalking across the fields or creeping around the woods. More often than not, I'll opt for my usual hunting boots along with an extra pair of thick socks to keep my toes safe from the frost.

A hat is a cold weather essential, and you'll probably want something a little more substantial than your usual hunting cap when there's a proper nip in the air. For the last few seasons, I've been using a brilliant fleece hat that provides great insulation, can be stretched down over my ears and even has a peak to help keep my face hidden from prying eyes. When I'm night shooting in extreme cold, I sometimes even step up to a ski hat.

Gloves also need to be upgraded for sub-zero hunting trips. The modern neoprene varieties are great and provide a good level of warmth without being too bulky. I always recommend the varieties with fold-back fingers, so you can uncover your trigger finger when you need to shoot. While it's impossible to predict the break point of your trigger when your fingers are numb with the cold, it's not much easier when they're wrapped up inside a glove. When it's really cold, I swap my usual winter gloves for a thick pair of woolly mittens. The whole front section of these mitts folds back to reveal fingerless gloves, so they provide excellent protection from the cold and enable me to expose my fingertips when it's time to shoot.

Another small and relatively inexpensive piece of clothing, which has made my winter hunting a lot more comfortable over the last few seasons, is a camouflage neck snood. This thick, fleecy tube is more compact than a scarf yet stops draughts from creeping down your neck and can also be pulled over your ears and up above your nose if you need extra protection or concealment.

Your local shooting shop should stock of variety of hats, gloves and snoods for you to peruse. If not, you'll find a massive selection at any of the bigger game fairs and online. These items aren't particularly expensive, yet make a tremendous difference on days when a cold easterly wind brings tears to your eyes. Get yourself properly kitted out and you'll be able to enjoy your shooting in the most unforgiving and most beautiful season of all.

# Recipes for winter

## PUB-STYLE PIGEON WITH MUSHROOMS AND RED WINE

The breast meat of a woodpigeon is regarded by chefs as some of the finest wild fare available. Dark, robust and full flavoured, it's a delicious meat that works very well with red wine.

This meaty pigeon dish tastes as good as steak and only takes about 10 minutes to cook. Serve it with chunky chips and peas for pub-grub dining in the comfort of your home.

*To serve 2*

### Ingredients

Breast meat from 2 woodpigeons, cut into 2cm chunks
1 large onion, chopped
6 or 7 medium-sized mushrooms, sliced
2 cloves of garlic, crushed
Red wine (about 1 glass)
A handful of plain flour
Knob of butter
Olive oil
Salt and pepper

Cut the pigeon breasts into 2cm chunks and roll in a handful of flour until evenly coated, then roughly chop the onion. Melt the butter in a large frying pan or wok along with about 2 tablespoons of olive oil. When the butter starts to foam, add the pigeon and fry until it begins to brown – this should take about 2 minutes. Then add the onion to the pan and gently fry for 2 or 3 minutes. When the onion begins to soften, crush in the garlic, add the sliced mushrooms and fry for another 2 or 3 minutes until the mushrooms become soft.

Pour a slosh of red wine (about 1 generous glass) into the pan to deglaze. Allow the wine to simmer for a few more minutes until it has reduced to a thick, dark gravy coating the pigeon and vegetables. Season with salt and pepper and serve.

## RABBIT WITH MUSTARD AND PRUNES

Prunes aren't just for constipated old fogies; they're a delicious, sugary dried fruit that works brilliantly with rabbit and mustard. And if they happen to keep you regular, better still.

The sugariness of the prunes and peppery warmth of the Dijon mustard gives this dish a mouth-watering sweet and sour taste, and it's a meal that's fresh enough to enjoy in the summer months while also being sufficiently hearty to satisfy the kind of hunger that cold winter weather brings on.

A useful little tip for evenly covering the rabbit pieces with flour (for this recipe and any other that requires the meat to be dusted) is to place them in a freezer bag and give them a good shake.

*To serve 4*

**Ingredients**
Best meat from 2 rabbits, cut into large chunks
1 tablespoon of flour
Olive oil
Knob of butter
1 large onion, finely chopped
225g prunes (the dried/stoned ones)
112g fromage frais
1 tablespoon of Dijon mustard
Salt and pepper

Cut the rabbit meat into large chunks and roll the pieces in flour to coat evenly. Heat the oil and butter in a large pan and then fry the rabbit pieces until golden brown. Add the prunes and chopped onion to the pan and pour over just enough water to cover. Season with a generous grind of salt and pepper, bring to the boil and turn down the heat to simmer gently for 45 minutes until the rabbit is tender.

Remove the rabbit with a slotted spoon and wrap in foil to keep warm. Stir the fromage frais and mustard into the pan and simmer gently for about 10 minutes until reduced to a creamy sauce. Spoon the sauce over the rabbit and serve. This dish is equally good served on a bed of rice or with mashed potato and crunchy greens.

## SPICED PIGEON BROTH

This lightly-spiced broth is a great winter warmer; the ideal supper to tuck into after an evening's roost shooting. You can serve it on rice but I prefer it with a couple of chunks of crusty bread.

Pigeon is a very dark, rich meat that stands up well to slow cooking techniques and holds its own against spicy flavours such as cumin. Frying the meat in the butter, shallot and garlic at the start infuses it with wonderful, sweet flavours.

*To serve 2*

### Ingredients

Breast meat from 2 woodpigeons, cut into 1-2cm cubes
2 medium potatoes, diced
2 medium parsnips, diced
2 large carrots, diced
4 shallots (or 1 large onion), finely chopped
1 clove of garlic
1 vegetable stock cube
Knob of butter
Half a teaspoon of ground cumin
570ml of water
Salt and pepper

Finely chop the shallots and roughly dice the carrots, parsnip and potatoes. Cut the pigeon breast meat into 1-2cm cubes.

Melt the knob of butter in a large saucepan; add the shallots and fry gently until soft. Then crush in the garlic clove, add the pigeon meat and fry for 3 or 4 minutes until it begins to turn brown.

Add the water and chopped vegetables and bring to the boil. Stir in the stock cube and the cumin and reduce the heat to a gentle simmer. Cover and cook for 45 minutes, stirring occasionally, until the vegetables become soft. The finished consistency should be that of a thick stew: not watery like a soup but still with enough cooking juice to cover the chunks in a thick sauce. Add salt and pepper to taste, and maybe a touch more cumin, then serve.

# LEGAL MATTERS AND KILL ZONES

## AIRGUN LAW

You do not need a licence to own an air rifle as long as its muzzle energy is below the 12ft.lb legal limit – and the onus is on you to ensure that it doesn't exceed that limit, whatever ammunition it's fed. Nonetheless, all airguns are classed as firearms in the eyes of the law and fall under the same control of firearms legislation. It is your responsibility to know this legislation and operate within it, as failure to do so could result in a court appearance with penalties ranging from hefty fines to life imprisonment.

At time of writing, current rules stated by the Home Office require airgun owners to abide by the following laws:

It is an offence for a person in possession of an air weapon to fail to take reasonable precautions to prevent someone under the age of 18 from gaining unauthorised access to it. A defence is provided where a person can show that they had reasonable grounds for believing the other person to be aged 18 or over.

It is an offence for a person under the age of 18 to purchase or hire an air weapon or ammunition for an air weapon.

It is an offence to sell, let on hire or make gift of an air weapon or ammunition for an air weapon to a person under the age of 18.

It is an offence for anyone under the age of 18 to have with them an air weapon or ammunition for an air weapon unless: they are under the supervision of a person aged 21 or over; they are shooting as a member of an approved target shooting club, or they are shooting at a shooting gallery and the only firearms being used are either air weapons or miniature rifles not exceeding .23 inch calibre, or the person is 14 years old or above and is on private premises with the consent of the occupier.

It is an offence to part with possession of an air weapon, or ammunition for an air weapon, to a person under the age of 18 except under the special circumstances mentioned immediately above.

It is an offence for any person shooting on private land, regardless of age, to use an air weapon for firing a pellet beyond the boundaries of the premises.

It is an offence for a supervising adult to allow a person under the age of 18 to use an air weapon for firing a pellet beyond the boundaries of premises.

It is an offence for any person to have an air weapon in a public place without a reasonable excuse. While there is no statutory definition of a reasonable excuse, it might include carrying a weapon to and from a shooting club, or taking a new weapon home from a dealer. However, it is ultimately for the courts to decide what a reasonable excuse is.

It is an offence to trespass with an air weapon, whether in a building or on land.

It is an offence to have an air weapon if you are prohibited from possessing a firearm. Anyone who has been sentenced to a custodial sentence of between three months and three years is prohibited from possessing an air weapon or other firearm or ammunition for five years from the date of their release. Anyone who has been sentenced to three years or more is prohibited for life.

It is an offence to fire an air weapon without lawful authority or excuse within 50 feet (15 metres) of the centre of a public road in such a way as to cause a road user to be injured, interrupted or endangered.

It is an offence to intentionally or recklessly kill certain wild animals and birds. When shooting live quarry, it is your responsibility to make sure that you only do so legally.

It is an offence to knowingly cause a pet animal to suffer unnecessarily, which could be committed by shooting at a pet animal.

It is an offence to have an air weapon with intent to damage or to destroy property. It is also an offence to have air weapons and be reckless as to whether property would be damaged or destroyed.

It is an offence to have an air weapon with intent to endanger life.

Although this legislation is accurate at the time of writing, it is your responsibility to ensure that you understand and abide by current laws relevant to the place where you live.

The above 'chapter and verse' sounds very prohibitive, as it is geared towards what you can't do rather than what you can. In simple terms, apart from some of the above mentioned exceptions, you can own an airgun if you are aged 18 and over – and you'll need to provide proof of age when you purchase one. For under-18s, it's a little more complicated as the law does not permit you to own an airgun, even if it is purchased for you by an adult. However, under-18s can use an airgun if supervised by someone aged 21 or over, and a person aged 14 and over can use an airgun unsupervised on land where they have been granted permission to shoot by an authorised person. However, the teenager can't transport the gun to that place unless supervised by an adult, so they'll have to get someone to escort them there, even if it's just a short walk along a country lane.

All airgun owners must ensure that their gun is stored in a way that prevents people aged under 18 from gaining access to it. The most secure method, and my choice, is the sort of lockable cabinet used for the storage of conventional rifles and shotguns. According to the Home Office, a suitably robust locking cupboard, with keys kept separate and secure, is also acceptable, as is a locking device that secures the gun to the fabric of the building.

You can shoot your air rifle on your own property (in a moderately sized garden, for example) although you'll be breaking the law the moment a pellet strays beyond your boundary. To shoot over ground that is not your own, you'll need the permission of the landowner or whoever is authorised to grant shooting permission – this may be a tenant farmer or gamekeeper. Whoever it is, make sure you receive written permission in case anyone ever challenges your right to be there. Wherever you shoot, the rule about keeping pellets within the permitted boundary always applies, so make sure you know where your shots will terminate whether they hit the intended target or not.

## INSURANCE FOR SHOOTERS

There is no legal requirement for airgun shooters to be insured but it is something that I would strongly recommend. A modest annual payment will insure you against damage or injury to machinery, buildings, livestock and people. Of course, it is every hunter's responsibility to ensure that an accident is never allowed to happen, but insurance provides peace of mind and will help to convince landowners that you have a professional attitude and take your shooting seriously.

Different insurers offer different premiums and I would suggest that you look closely at what you get for your money rather than just opting for the cheapest. I have been a member of the BASC (British Association for Shooting and Conservation) for many years and think they provide a great service – to me and shooting as a whole. This organisation works hard to protect and promote the importance of country sports and their benefits to the natural world. As well as including comprehensive insurance cover, membership of the BASC entitles you to free advice from the organisation's numerous experts in every imaginable field of shooting, and you also get their regular magazine. The BASC is a respected and trusted organisation that most landowners will have heard of. I'm afraid the same cannot be said for some of the cheaper providers.

The premiums charged by the better insurers are still relatively small compared with the price we pay for our hardware, and I'm convinced that they represent good value. I once made the mistake of buying very cheap insurance in my early days as a hunter and, judging by the difficulty they had trying to get my membership card to me, I wasn't left with much confidence in their ability to provide a professional service.

## LEGITIMATE QUARRY

The hunter's duty to act within the law also includes knowing what quarry we can legally pursue. It is also vital to have a good reason to justify the taking of life. The decision to kill an animal is not something to be taken lightly, and should be based on sound reason and never the loutish desire to simply have a go at live quarry.

Killing an animal that is not recognised as legitimate quarry is not just unacceptable, it's illegal and could land you in dire trouble. Therefore, all hunters must be able to quickly and confidently identify their quarry species. If there's ever the least shadow of a doubt, don't take the shot – it's too late once you've pulled the trigger. Reckless shooting not only jeopardises your own right to enjoy the sport but also that of the responsible majority. The conduct of shooters is always under the spotlight and we should all strive to act as good ambassadors for our fine sport – all of the time.

An interest in country sports is likely to result in a comprehensive collection of wildlife books. These volumes will serve as a reasonable grounding when it comes to quarry identification but nothing beats first-hand observation. With most elements of shooting, the best way to learn is to get out there and experience it, and that certainly applies to the observation of wildlife. Not only will studying wild creatures help you to clearly distinguish legitimate quarry, it will also help you to understand and predict their behaviour when you venture out with the gun. The ideal way to really accelerate this learning curve is to befriend an experienced countryman and learn from him. Better still if you can accompany him on his forays and share first-hand his knowledge of animals, plants and their habitat. Knowledge gained through years of close contact with the natural world is invaluable so should be gratefully received from anyone who is willing to share it.

Getting back to legal quarry, the main pest species the UK air rifle hunter can target all year round with no restriction are the brown rat, the grey squirrel and the rabbit. Others, including the mink, might be targeted with FAC-rated air rifles.

Authorisation to shoot avian quarry (birds) with an air rifle is granted under general license by the government body Natural England. Rather than actually obtaining them as you might a fishing licence, general licences are a set of rules that must be adhered to if you're going to stay on the right side of the law. Although you do not need to carry a paper copy of the relevant general licence, it is a legal obligation to read, understand and comply with its conditions.

Species of bird listed under the general licence that can be regarded as legitimate quarry include woodpigeon, feral pigeon, collared dove, crow, magpie, jay, rook and jackdaw. Ring-necked and monk parakeets, which have formed large colonies in the wild that are causing considerable crop damage, also appear on the current general licence. The list goes on to include the Canada goose, Egyptian goose, ruddy duck and lesser black-backed gull, but these are not generally considered as air rifle quarry species.

In very simple terms, the licence permits authorised persons (landowners and the people to whom they grant permission to shoot) the right to control the above bird species in order to prevent the spread of disease or serious damage to livestock, foodstuffs for livestock, crops, vegetables, fruit, growing timber, fisheries or inland waters. Under the general licence, the feral pigeon is the only avian pest that can be shot using artificial lighting. It is, therefore, illegal to shoot any of the others by lamplight.

The general licence also states that the pests it lists should be killed in a quick and humane manner. This should be the aim of any responsible hunter targeting any live quarry.

Natural England's general licence goes on to state that people acting under its guidelines must be satisfied that non-lethal methods of resolving the problem posed by pests are ineffective or impracticable. As far as I'm aware, there is no definitive explanation of what amounts to 'ineffective or impracticable' and for this reason this lack of clarity has been criticised by shooting organisations.

Regardless of any supposed grey areas within the wording of Natural England's general licence, failure to comply with its requirements can carry a fine of up to £5,000 and/or a six-month custodial sentence, so be warned. And remember that the terms of the licence are frequently reviewed so make sure you keep up to date with them. You can familiarise yourself with the relevant documents, chapter and verse, by visiting www.naturalengland.org.uk

The list of species deemed as pests varies from country to country, and the above only applies to England at the time of writing. To be sure of current legislation on the control of pests where you live, check the website of the relevant government agency or seek clarification from one of the official organisations that represents shooters in your locality.

Ultimately, the final decision of what amounts to lawful and ethical pest control is up to you to decide for the varying scenarios you are presented with. To make the right decision, carefully read and understand the legal requirements and then apply those rules to pest control situations as you encounter them.

## KILL ZONES

Throughout the various hunting scenarios described in this book, I have alluded to the sort of shots the hunter is likely to take depending on how his quarry presents itself. When it comes to where you should aim to land your pellet, it is difficult to lay down hard and fast rules: the simple answer is wherever it is likely to cause the most damage and result in a clean kill.

Wounding is something that any hunter with a grain of integrity will strive to avoid. At best, it results in the need to take a rapid follow-up shot (preferably after running in to get the muzzle close to your quarry's head). At worst, it results in the wounded creature escaping to suffer a lingering death.

Knowing exactly where to place a shot depends on an understanding of your quarry's anatomy. The decision is based on the whereabouts of its vital organs – the heart, lungs and brain – and how to drive your pellet into them depending on the angle of the shot and the presentation of your target. The significance of striking a vital organ should always be borne in mind and remember that a 'body shot' (a reckless attempt to connect with the largest area presented) does not constitute a heart-and-lung shot, which needs to be carefully calculated.

My advice to newcomers to the sport is to become a proficient shot on paper targets before going out in pursuit of live quarry. When you become competent enough to achieve the required standard of accuracy with confidence from a variety of stances, you can then move on to hunting. In the early days, I would suggest that you endeavour to get as close as possible to your quarry and restrict yourself to head shots. Admittedly, such a shot requires a high standard of accuracy, but it carries a much-reduced risk of wounding. A direct hit will result in a clean dispatch, a low miss is likely to cause a fatal strike to the neck and a misplaced shot to the left, right or over the top should pass harmlessly wide of the mark.

When shooting rabbits, head shots are best taken when the target is presented side-on. From this angle, you have a kill area of around 30mm between the eye and ear. The head of a rabbit also presents a slightly smaller, though equally effective, kill zone when viewed from behind. It's quite a small target when the rabbit is squat down (so you'll need to be relatively close to hit it) but it is much better presented when the rabbit is sat upright and alert. Many hunters successfully manage to achieve clean kills by shooting rabbits with heart-and-lung shots. I prefer to stick to the head, even when using an FAC-rated airgun.

I also prefer head shots when targeting squirrels. Again, my favoured strike area is between the eye and ear. This kill area is slightly smaller than that presented by the rabbit but still represents a substantial target. Squirrels can also be cleanly killed when shot in the heart-and-lung area, though how to reach it varies greatly depending on the angles involved. Generally speaking, if a squirrel is presented side-on and is standing on all fours, I aim to land my shot just behind and a fraction below the shoulder of the front leg. Preferably, the shot will be taken with my unsuspecting quarry facing slightly away from me (not a common opportunity as squirrels tend to face towards anything that poses a threat) as this enables the pellet to drive in behind and through a larger part of the heart-and-lung area. If the squirrel is sat upright and facing towards you, an equally effective shot can be delivered through the chest. I prefer this shot at an upward angle with the squirrel presented slightly to the side, when a strike just between and slightly behind the elbow and shoulder will connect with the vital organs. Squirrels also offer a very effective kill zone when they cling tight to tree trunks, showing only their back. At this angle, a solid strike to the spinal column, from just below the shoulders up to the rear of the skull, will produce a clean kill.

Despite their verminous reputation, rats deserve the same respect as all other quarry when it comes to the right to a swift death. The heart-and-lung area, accessed from just behind the shoulder when presented side-on, is a dependable kill zone but I still rely mostly on head shots. Most of my rat shooting is done over ranges of less than 20 metres, and often half that, so connecting with the skull is easily achievable when taking rested shots.

The kill areas for avian species generally depend on the size of your quarry, yet I still favour head shots. As previously described, it is a small target but modern airguns are very accurate tools and it's just a matter of getting close enough to be able to shoot within your own limitations.

I'm not an advocate of chest shots on larger avian pests, such as carrion crows and woodpigeons. These are sturdy birds and the breastplate and muscle that cover it provide a tough shield that airgun pellets struggle to penetrate, especially when using a gun producing power within the 12ft.lb, non-FAC, legal limit. However, if the chest is tilted away at a slight sideward angle, there is a less obstructed route to the heart-and-lung area if you can land the pellet just in front of the elbow of the wing. Better still, wait until avian quarry is facing away from you and a hit between the shoulders will arrive at the vital organs with minimal obstruction from bone and tissue. This shot works best at flatter or downward angles and should not be used when taking steep upward shots that don't present the correct angle of penetration.

Small avian pests, such as collared doves, magpies and jays, can be cleanly killed with a solid strike to the chest from the front. The damage caused by a direct hit to their small bodies will be fatal – but it has to be direct. I favour this shot at closer ranges so I can ensure that the target is hit squarely and the pellet will find the vital organs.

It's difficult to discuss kill areas without venturing into the .177 versus .22 calibre debate. In my opinion, the extra clout provided by the bigger, heavier .22 round provides more margin for error: its additional impact simply causes more damage even if it strays slightly wide of the intended mark. For this reason, I generally recommend that newcomers opt for .22 and concentrate on getting close. However, hefty .22 pellets have a very pronounced trajectory when compared with the flatter flight path of the zippy little .177 projectile. At longer ranges, considerable hold-over must be given to the shot to compensate for the drop of the .22 before the .177 has strayed more than a centimetre below its original zero. I believe that when shooting sub-12ft.lb airguns, the .177 has the potential for greater accuracy at longer ranges. The trouble is that the improved accuracy comes with the cost of a reduced kill area as a result of the lesser impact: a .177 pellet must strike a vital organ directly to cause a clean kill. When all is said and done, both calibres have their pros and cons, so there is very little to choose between them. If you've already made your choice and are content with it, I would suggest that you stick with whatever it is and concentrate more on pellet selection and good shooting technique, which will stand you in good stead whatever calibre you choose.

At present, I think I've found something close to the best of both worlds in the shape of a .22 FAC-rated airgun producing just under 30ft.lb. But even this comes at a cost: apart from the hassle and expense of the licensing process, there are great restrictions on its use. The additional power is often a blessing as it gives me a fairly flat-shooting airgun with all the wallop of .22 calibre – although I rarely use it at ranges much beyond those I'd hunt at with a legal limit airgun. Unfortunately, the extra grunt is sometimes a curse. For starters, there's no way I'd ever use it around enclosed farm buildings, so the freedom that accounts for much of the charm of air-gunning is immediately lost. You simply can't have it all.

# PREPARING MEAT FOR THE TABLE

## HANGING

As far as I'm concerned, there's no point in hanging shot quarry that's destined for the table.

Although the tradition of hanging game does 'develop' the flavour, I wouldn't go as far as to say it improves it. Wild meat tastes relatively strong in the first place, especially when compared with the pallid stuff you buy in the supermarket, so I don't see any point in leaving it to putrefy so the flavour becomes even stronger. In fact, the main reason why a lot of people believe they don't like game is because they've only tasted it when it has been left to hang for too long. They would probably have found the same meat to be delicious if they'd had it fresh from the field.

My advice is to prepare meat for the table as quickly as is practical. If you don't intend to eat it for a while, simply bag it up, label it and put it in the freezer where it will keep for months.

## PIGEON PREPARATION

Preparing a woodpigeon for the table is an incredibly simple task. The breast makes up the majority of the meat on a pigeon, so there's little point in going through the rigmarole of plucking and drawing the bird – all you want is the breast meat.

Begin by plucking the feathers from around the breast until the area around the breast muscles and just under the wings is clear. Pigeons have very loose feathers that come away easily, so plucking this patch isn't a difficult job.

With the breast area clear of feathers, pinch up the skin in the centre and make a cut so you can peel it away from the dark breast meat and pull it back to beneath the wings. Then, cut down into one side of the breast, starting at the top of the hard central ridge of bone that runs down the front of the breastplate. Continue the cut down along the ridge, paring the meat away from the bone down to the bottom of the breast, up under the wing and back to where you started. You should now have one large, heart-shaped chunk of breast meat. Repeat with the other side of the breast, rinse to remove any stray feathers and it's ready for the table.

Use the same technique for collared doves, and even for rooks if you're tempted to use the breast meat from young branchers in a pie.

## RABBIT PREPARATION

The method of preparing rabbits for the table is somewhat more involved than that for pigeons, and it begins in the field.

When you retrieve a shot rabbit, its bladder should be emptied to prevent the urine from tainting the meat. Simply hold the bunny head-up with its body dangling, and slide your other hand down its belly while giving a gentle squeeze in a downward stroke to squirt out the remnants of its last drink.

Removing the guts from rabbits (usually referred to as 'paunching') is another job that's best done in the field. Here, you can leave the entrails in some discreet place where they'll be devoured by foxes and badgers rather than having to dispose of them at home.

Place the rabbit on its back and pinch up the loose flesh where the belly starts just below the ribcage and make a small cut crossways. Keeping the skin raised, slide the blade back inside the slit at a shallow angle (to avoid puncturing the intestines) and make a cut down towards the vent to expose the guts. At this point I lift the rabbit by its hind legs and give it a bit of a jolt to help the guts on their way out. Then I push two or three fingers of my free hand up into the slit, right up behind the ribcage, and draw all of the innards down and out. And that's it, the rabbit is paunched.

The next job is skinning. I find that this task is easier done at home with a very sharp little knife. There are advantages to doing it in the field – it certainly eliminates the risk of taking fleas into your car or house – but I prefer skinning at home, on a decent work surface and equipped with that razor-sharp knife, a robust chopping board, a cleaver and a pair of kitchen scissors.

I begin by using the cleaver to chop off the hind and front legs around the knee joint (there's hardly any meat beneath there) and remove the head. If you don't have a cleaver, snap the legs at the joints to break the bone, then slice them off with a sharp knife, and leave the head until later.

Next, peel the skin away from the meat at the belly and push your fingers around towards the back until you can reach right through around the rabbit's waist; at this stage the skin will still be connected at the front and back, forming a sort of 'handle' in the middle. Push the hind legs up through the skin while pulling back at the 'handle' to peel the meat and skin apart. Keeping going until the rear section of the skin is removed. Once you've popped the back half of the rabbit out of its fur coat, grip just in front of the hind legs with one hand and pull off the rest of the skin in one swift, forward stroke with your other hand. If you removed the head with a cleaver, the whole skin will come right away. If you left the head on, pull the skin until it reaches the top of the neck, then lay the rabbit back on the board and cut off its head with a sharp carving knife – it's much easier to slice through the neck with the fur out of the way. Next, make cuts either side of the tail so you can twist it off later.

Place the skinned rabbit on its back with its hind legs towards you and extend the original belly slit right down to the end of the pelvis. Push the hind legs apart, and then place the blade of your knife along the pelvis so the point is facing the front end of the rabbit. Now slam the base of your hand down onto the back of the knife. The stiff blow will enable you to open the tract around the vent and remove any remains of the genitals, anus and intestines – often along with a few droppings – as you twist out the tail. Rinse your rabbit under a cold tap and it's ready for the pot.